Seeds of Hope

Seeds of Hope

Dr. K. Parameswaran
Namboothiri,
M.D (Ayu)

MOTILAL BANARSIDASS
INTERNATIONAL
DELHI

First Edition : Delhi, 2026

ISBN : 978-93-47683-79-4

Also available at :

MOTILAL BANARSIDASS INTERNATIONAL

41 U.A. Bungalow Road, (Back Lane) Jawahar Nagar, Delhi-110007
4261/3 (Basement), Ansari Road, Darya Ganj, New Delhi-110002
Shop#. 6, 241, Luz Ginza Complex, Luz Corner, Mylapore, Chennai - 600004
12/1A, 2nd Floor, Bankim Chatterjee Street, Kolkata - 700073

Stockist : Motilal Books, Ashok Rajpath, Near Kali Mandir, Patna-800004

Printed in India by
MOTILAL BANARSIDASS INTERNATIONAL

Blessings

With utmost reverence and heartfelt gratitude, I bow to divine Mother, whose blessings have been the guiding light and eternal source of strength throughout this journey. It is by her boundless grace that this humble work has come to fruition. I dedicate this endeavour at her lotus feet, praying that her benevolent presence may forever illuminate and bless my thoughts, words, and deeds, now and always.

तव स्तन्यं मन्ये धरणिधरकन्ये हृदयतः
पयः पारावारः परिवहति सारस्वतमिव।
दयावत्या दत्तं द्रविडशिशुरास्वाद्य तव यत्
कवीनां प्रौढानामजनि कमनीयः कवयिता।

औं अमृतेश्वर्यै नमः

Foreword

It's my immense pleasure to write the foreword for the book "SEEDS OF HOPE" authored by Dr. K. Parameswaran. Dr. Namboothiri's book towards integrating classical Ayurvedic knowledge with contemporary clinical insights is very appreciable. Male infertility is emerging as a significant health concern in the contemporary era which demands both scientific and compassionate understanding.

Dr. Namboothiri has diligently drawn insights from ancient Ayurvedic texts, clinical experience, and current researches to present the concept of male infertility clearly. This work highlights the classical aspects of Shukra Dhatu and its disorders and also interpret them into clinically applicable form suited to modern contexts.

I am confident that this book will be invaluable to postgraduate students, clinicians, and researchers engaged in reproductive health and Ayurvedic management.

I congratulate Dr. Parameswaran Namboothiri, for his notable academic contribution and extend my best wishes for the book's success and its positive impact on the Ayurvedic medical community globally.

- Swamy Sankaramritananda Puri. M.D (Ayu)

Dean, Amrita School of Ayurveda
Amrita Vishwa Vidyapeetham
Amritapuri, Kollam, Kerala

Foreword

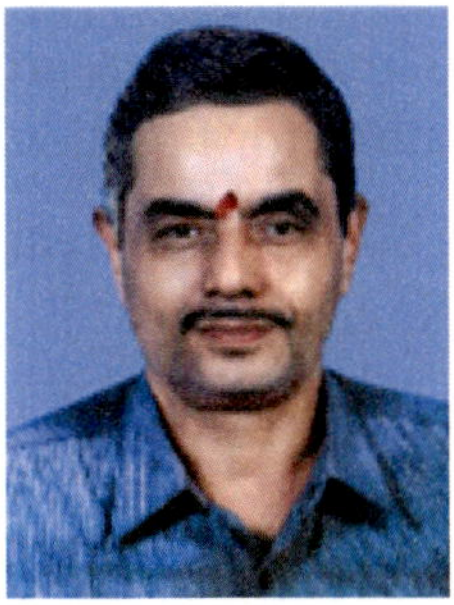

It is with immense pride and admiration that I write this foreword for my son's remarkable book, "SEEDS OF HOPE" a significant contribution to the field of male infertility. Having served as a District Medical Officer for years, I have witnessed the profound challenges couples face with reproductive difficulties. Male infertility remains an underappreciated aspect of life and this book fills a vital gap in managing male infertility.

In my medical career, I have observed our understanding of male reproductive health, from basic clinical observations to the sophisticated use of advanced diagnostic tools and therapeutic interventions. My son's work may stand at the forefront of this progress, providing a clear, evidence-based insights that blend academic scholarship with practical clinical implementations. "SEEDS OF HOPE" is more than a book; it is a hope for countless couples seeking answers and solutions. It highlights not only the years of dedicated research and clinical experience but also a passionate commitment to improve the lives of those affected by male infertility.

I appreciate my son for his determination and scholarly integrity in bringing this great work to reality. I am confident that this book will serve as an invaluable resource for clinicians, researchers, and patients, helping to foster a new hope for families around the world.

With great appreciation and best wishes for its success,

- Dr. G. K. Namboothiri

Retired District Medical Officer
Indian Systems of Medicine (ISM)

Preface

This book focuses on what can actually be done for men struggling with infertility in day-to-day practice. Rather than becoming a purely theoretical discourse on Vandhyata, the emphasis has been given to the practical aspects of assessment, planning, and execution of Ayurvedic management in a clinical setting.

Theoretical references from classical texts and contemporary literature have been included only where they illuminate and support practical decision-making, not for the sake of completeness alone. Each concept has been selected and presented with the question in mind: "How will this help the practitioner sitting with a couple in distress and limited time, resources, and options?"

Wherever possible, clinical data from actual practice have been incorporated to demonstrate the significant changes observed in seminal parameters, symptomatology, and fertility outcomes following Ayurvedic interventions. These data are not offered as grand claims, but as honest reflections of what can be achieved when foundational principles are applied with care, individualisation, and adherence to ethical and clinical standards.

Every chapter concludes with a concise summary of the key points discussed, allowing the reader to consolidate learning and quickly revisit the central ideas and protocols. This structure is intended to give students, teachers, and clinicians a comprehensive yet accessible feel of the subject, so that the book can be used both for systematic study and for quick reference in clinical practice.

This work is the outcome of years of clinical exposure, academic engagement, and iteraction with patients, students, and colleagues who continually inspired deeper inquiry into the neglected area of male infertility. With great cherishment and humility, this book is presented before all well-wishers, teachers, students, peers, and the many couples whose journeys have shaped its pages, in the hope that it will become a small but meaningful aid in restoring confidence, dignity, and the joy of parenthood to those who seek help.

- Dr. K. Parameswaran Namboothiri

Professor & Head,
Department of Panchakarma
Amrita School of Ayurveda,
Amrita Vishwa Vidyapeetham
Amritapuri, Kerala.

Acknowledgement

With utmost reverence and heartfelt gratitude, this humble work submit at the lotus feet of the Divine Mother, whose boundless grace has served as the guiding light and eternal source of strength throughout this entire journey, praying that She may forever illuminate the path ahead, blessing every thought with clarity, every word with truth, and every deed with compassion now and always.

This book is the fulfilment of a long-nurtured dream, and it would not have been possible without the love, guidance, and support of my dear ones.

First and foremost, deepest gratitude to my beloved father Dr. G. Kesavan Namboothiri and mother Smt. Saraswathi, who laid the foundation of my values, encouraged every aspiration, and stood by me through every phase of this journey with unconditional love and blessings. Their quiet sacrifices and constant prayers have been the invisible strength behind each page of this work.

Heartfelt gratitude to my wife Neenu Devika, whose patience, understanding, and unwavering faith sustained me through long hours of writing, clinical work, and research. Her companionship and silent support, often at the cost of her own comforts, have been an anchor in times of fatigue and doubt.

To my son Kesavan and daughter Aparna, thank you for filling my life with joy and reminding me of the purpose behind this endeavour. Their affection, innocent questions, and gentle tolerance of my frequent absence from family moments have been a source of inspiration and renewed energy.

Warm thanks to my elder and younger brothers Govindan and Narayanan and their families, whose encouragement, affection, and constant moral support have always surrounded me like an extended circle of strength. Their words of appreciation and belief in my abilities have made this path lighter and more meaningful.

With profound reverence, this acknowledgement is also dedicated to all my teachers, from nursery school to postgraduate and research mentors, who shaped my understanding of Ayurveda, clinical thinking, and the ethics of medical practice. Their teachings and example continue to guide every decision and line written in this book.

My sincere acknowledgements to each patient who consented to participate, who bore with the inconveniences of follow-up visits, investigations, and detailed questioning, and who continued to believe in the healing potential of Ayurveda. Their trust not only allowed the documentation of meaningful clinical outcomes, but also transformed routine practice into a rich field of learning that could be systematised and shared for the benefit of many others.

I extend my heartfelt gratitude to Mr. Aravind. G. Namboothiri for his excellent design of the cover page, which beautifully captures the essence of "Seeds of Hope" and elevates its visual appeal for readers in Ayurvedic research, clinical practice and common man.

Heartfelt thanks are extended to my friends and colleagues at Amrita School of Ayurveda, whose support has been instrumental through every stage of this book. Their invaluable suggestions, shared expertise, and unwavering encouragement transformed a cherished dream into a tangible reality.

I sincerely acknowledge my students for their continuous support and valuable inputs through constant discussions, which greatly helped in refining this work.

I extend profound gratitude to Motilal Banarsidass for their unwavering support and exemplary cooperation, which proved instrumental in ensuring the timely completion of this scholarly work.

Content

Blessings (*v*)
Foreword by Swamy Sankaramritananda Puri (*vii*)
Foreword by Dr. G. K. Namboothiri (*ix*)
Preface (*xi*)
Acknowledgement (*xiii*)

Chapter-1 : Introduction 1
Chapter-2 : Concepts of Male Reproductive Physiology in Ayurveda 10
Chapter-3 : Etiology and Classification of Male Infertility 20
Chapter-4 : Clinical Features and Diagnosis 37
Chapter-5 : Treatment Principles in Ayurveda 46
Chapter-6 : Panchakarma and Detoxification Protocols in Male Infertility 53
Chapter-7 : Dietetics and Lifestyle (Āhāra & Vihāra) in Male Infertility 61
Chapter-8 : Psychosocial, Behavioural and Supportive Interventions 68
Chapter-9 : Case Studies and Clinical Protocols 79
Chapter-10 : Research Updates and Evidence Synthesis 90
Chapter-11 : Discussion 103
Chapter-12 : Conclusion 114

Appendices *120*

Chapter - 1

Introduction

1.1. Background

The need to procreate and exist to carry on the line is one of the basic human needs. This was considered by our Acharyas, as a strong motivator, that was closely associated with the health, longevity, and social wellbeing. Maharshi Caraka says that the one who leaves healthy progenies behind never dies, underlining the reproduction as one of the key purposes of life.

More couples are however finding it difficult to conceive in the modern clinical practice. Male factor infertility is becoming a significant and largely unrecognised cause amongst them. Meanwhile, contemporary lifestyles typified by stress, sedentary lifestyles, environmental toxins and distorted eating behaviours still have an adverse impact on the reproductive health of men.

The book presents male infertility, more so, oligospermia, in a two-sided way: the most recent andrological knowledge on the one hand, and the conceptual and therapeutic Ayurvedic tradition rich as it is on the other. It is founded on a protocol-based clinical study, case-based documentation, and a critical review of classical literature and modern studies.

1.2. Definition of infertility and male infertility

The traditional definition of infertility is the inability of a couple to become pregnant after one year of frequent unprotected sex. In the situation when the leading cause of such failure is in the male partner, one refers to male infertility. The contemporary Androgenology measures the male fertility in a large part by taking samples of semen. The lower limit of semen characteristics in healthy men according to the World Health Organization (2010) reference values is;

- Sperm concentration ≥ 15 million/mL
- Total sperm count ≥ 39 million per ejaculate
- Total motility ≥ 40% with progressive motility ≥ 32%
- Normal morphology ≥ 4%
- Vitality ≥ 58%
- Deviation from these parameters gives rise to descriptive diagnostic labels:
- Oligospermia / Oligozoospermia – sperm concentration < 15 million/mL
- Asthenozoospermia – reduced progressive motility (< 32–40%)
- Teratozoospermia – increased proportion of morphologically abnormal sperm (> 96% abnormal forms)
- Azoospermia – complete absence of spermatozoa in ejaculate

In this work, particular emphasis is placed on oligospermia, which in Ayurvedic terms is closely comparable to *kṣīṇa śukra*—the state of diminished or debilitated seminal dhātu.

1.3. Epidemiology and contemporary trends

International estimates indicate that infertility occurs in 8 to 12 percent of couples where male causes are estimated as 30 to 40 percent.

One of the troubling tendencies that have been observed in the past decades is the loss of sperm concentration and motility among the general male population. The reports in androgenic literature indicate that the average number of sperm has depleted significantly within the past fifty years whereas motility has decreased as compared to previous standards of 60-70 percent to approximately 30-40 percent in most series.

Several factors contribute to this deterioration:

- Environmental exposures to heat, industrial chemicals, pesticides and heavy metals
- Lifestyle issues such as obesity, smoking, alcohol, recreational drugs and stress
- Systemic diseases (diabetes, hypertension, cardiovascular disease)
- Varicocele, genital tract infections and other local pathologies
- Genetic and endocrine disorders affecting spermatogenesis

It is important to note that as many as 90 percent of infertility in men can be due to low sperm count, low motility, abnormal morphology, or a combination of these; however, a direct identifiable cause is not found in most of the individuals and this is termed as idiopathic.

It is on this basis that there is a pressing need of therapeutic measures which are safe, cost effective and can enhance the quality of sperm and general health particularly in idiopathic and functional cases.

1.4. Rationale for an Ayurvedic approach

According to Ayurveda, reproduction is the balancing act of four factors namely: Rtu (good time), Ksetra (optimal reproductive tract), Bija (clean and strong gametes) and Ambu (sufficient nutrient milieu). Interruption in any of them may result to infertility. Male infertility is mainly a manifestation of derangement of bijas and dhathus that support it.

A number of arguments favour the study of Ayurveda in male infertility:

Holistic view of śukra dhatu

Though sperm is not just the visible semen but the ultimate and the most exquisite product of all dhataus. Its health is a sign of the wholeness of the whole nutritive chain - food intake to tissue formation. Therefore, Ayurvedic management of male infertility has to do with restoration of digestion (agni), metabolism and balance of systemic doṣa, not local semen parameters only.

Doṣa-based understanding of kṣīṇa śukra

Classical descriptions make ksani shukra of Vata and Pitta predominant vitiation. This offers a conceptual perspective of contemporary state into which oligospermia, asthenozoospermia and ejaculatory disorders can be interpreted as a single pathophysiological model.

Emphasis on Śodhana and Rasāyana–Vajīkaraṇa

Conservative texts prescribe a series of Pañcakarma (bio purificatory treatments) with Rasasayana and Vajikarana treatment to replenish the quality and quantity of sukra. The reasoning is simple: with the removal of āma (metabolic toxins) and the cleansing of srotas (tissues), the action of rejuvenative medicines are improved.

Personalisation and long-term safety

Based on Ayurvedic prescriptions, interventions are customized to each person constitution (prakriti), disease stage, strength and comorbidities, and with mostly herbal and ghritta-based preparations, which have a good safety profile when used correctly.

Addressing psychosocial dimensions

Ayurveda identifies the importance of manas (mind) in reproduction, recognises that grief, fear, anxiety and loss of self-esteem have the potential to worsen sexual dysfunction and infertility. The therapeutic plan includes lifestyle regulation, counselling, yoga and meditation, which have provided the psychosomatic approach which is frequently lacking in the normal biomedical practice.

Given these strengths, integrating Ayurvedic principles with modern diagnostics offers a promising, yet under-utilised, avenue for managing male infertility.

1.5. Ancient references: Caraka, Suśruta and other Saṃhitās

Classical Āyurvedic texts provide descriptions of male reproductive physiology and disorders affecting virility and fertility

- Caraka Saṃhita speaks of the Sukra dhatu as the nature of all dhatus whose weakening (kshina) results in such characteristics as sexual debility, infertile and loss of enthusiasm. It defines such illnesses as klaibya (impotence) and aprajatva (infertility) and prescribes treatment under Rasasayana and Vajikarana to increase the progeny.

- Suśruta Saṃhita expounds on the anatomy of the male reproductive organs such as sukravaha srotas with mule in testes (vrsna) and medhra (penis). Damage to these structures is reported to result in such malformations as sterility and loss of sexual function, showing the significance of clean channels for healthy flow of śukra.
- There is further systematisation of classifications of śukra doṣa in Aṣhtanga Hrdaya and portents of various formulations like ghrita, lehya, curna, kashaya, taila etc. to enhance quantity, quality, consistency, colour and smell of sukra, which are similar to modern day parameters of semen.

Notably, the following pages all refer to the use of protocol-like sequences: Dīpana–Pācana to fire up Agni, Snehana–Swedana to lubricate the body, Shodhana (in particular, virecana and basti) to expel vitiated doṣas, and then Rasāyana and Vājikaraṇa drugs to nourish śukra and bring fertility.

These literary bases are the foundations of the therapeutic regimen investigated in the current study.

1.6. Contemporary and modern research review

In recent decades a scientific interest in Ayurvedic and other traditional treatments of male infertility has been increasing. In summary of the literature survey as presented in the current study, it has been shown:

- Over 200 clinical and experimental works on aphrodisiac (Vajikarana) therapies.

- Approximately 50 articles specifically focus on oligospermia or male subfertility using different single drugs or compound preparations.

These involve using Māṣa-aśvagandhādi cūrṇa, many ghṛita preparations, uttara basti, rasāyana yogas and other classical preparations, which usually report improvements in semen parameters and subjective sexual activity. However, several gaps remain:

1. **Lack of integrated, protocol-based interventions**

   Most studies have focused on single formulations or limited interventions, without combining systematic Pañcakarma with follow-up Vajīkaraṇa regimes as recommended in the Saṃhitās.

2. **Small sample sizes and methodological limitations**

   Many studies are uncontrolled, with small sample population and inadequate statistical analysis, limiting the generalisability of their findings.

3. **Insufficient emphasis on objective semen parameters**

   While some reports document sperm count and motility, fewer provide comprehensive semen analysis using contemporary WHO criteria or long-term follow-up on conception rates.

4. **Minimal integration with modern diagnostic work-up**

   Very few studies systematically document hormonal profiles, imaging, andrology evaluations and exclusion of confounding pathologies such as varicocele, STDs or endocrine disorders.

Conversely, the current work is in patients of oligospermia who were well-screened in terms of:

- Standard modern investigations and WHO semen analysis was done at baseline and at periodic follow-ups.
- A composite regimen was employed, comprising of Dīpana-Pācana, Snehapana, Virecana, Yoga basti with Sukra janana gana kwatha and Mahanarayana taila, then internally shukra shodhana and vajikarana yogas such as Shukra shodhana gana lehya and Vanarivati.
- Outcomes were measured both in relation to the change in the parameters of semen as well as in relation to clinical conception as described in the detailed case series where all the three couples were successful in getting pregnant after completing the protocol.
- Therefore, this current monograph is poised to occupy an important gap with the provision of a theoretical synthesis, as well as a practice-based, evidence-based protocol on the Ayurvedic approach to manage male infertility.

1.7. Aims and structure of this book

Building upon the classical foundations and contemporary clinical research outlined above, this book aims to:

1. Clarify the conceptual basis of male reproductive physiology and infertility from both modern and Ayurvedic viewpoints.
2. Present a detailed, replicable protocol of Pañcakarma and Vajīkaraṇa therapy for oligospermia and related conditions, with clear indications, contraindications and procedural steps.

3. Showcase clinical evidence through systematically documented case studies and study results demonstrating improvements in semen parameters and conception outcomes.
4. Integrate diet, lifestyle and psychosocial considerations into a holistic management plan for the infertile couple.

Chapter - 2

Concepts of Male Reproductive Physiology In Ayurveda

2.1 Background Information

Ayurveda introduces the male reproductive system as an expression of a deeply connected combination of the body nourishment, metabolism, the mental state, and the doṣha balance. In Ayurveda, rather than looking at the physiology of reproduction primarily in anatomical terms and in hormone-mediated processes, fertility is viewed as a manifestation of the integrity of dhatu-parinama the gradual refinement of tissues culminating in the finest and most important body essence, the Śukra Dhatu. This śukra does not restrict itself to the ejaculated seminal fluid; but it is the climax of health and vitality in the system.[1] The health of all the tissues that come before is directly dependent on the condition of śukra, which directly affects strength, virility, enthusiasm, immunity, and the ability to give healthy progeny[2].

The classical texts present in the Saṃhita show that our Acharyas knew that śukra was a reproductive and systemic energy. This chapter will examine the nature, formation, and functions of sperm, which is known as sukra dhatu, and how this can be related to the reproductive physiology.

2.2 Śukra Dhātu and Reproductive Tissue Health

The importance of Sukra Dhatu among the seven dhatus is that, it is the last result of total tissue finesse. It is the strongest, the nourishing and life-giving substance in the body. According to Ayurveda, the essence of all the dhatus is called as sukra and it only becomes possible when the metabolic change of each of the preceding dhatus is ideal and unhindered. Being the terminal dhatu in the metabolic chain, its quality indicates the general health of the body of the individual, both physically, psychologically and reproductively. According to classical explanations, there are two forms of sperm: the subtle form (avyakta śukra), which is spread throughout the body, making one feel vital, strong, complex-colored, joyful and Ojas-of-a-like activities; the visible sperm (vyakta śukra), which is the ejaculated seminal fluid involved in direct reproduction.[3]

To be healthy, the previous dhātu, rasa, rakta, māṃsa, medas, asthi, and majjā, has to be nourished correctly. When any tissue is too weak, or improperly developed, śukra will be deficient in quantity, of bad quality, or is incapable of its functions. The state of agni (metabolic fire) and the flow of nutrients via srotases (channels) is a decisive factor in the purification of śukra. The weak digestion leads to the formation of amas and the blockage of the pathways, which is not able to convert dhātus into the right form and finally results in poor quality of śukra[4]. This is associated with the current state of reproductive pathology when hormonal imbalance, nutritional deficiencies, and metabolic disorders disrupt the process of sperm formation and seminal quality.

According to the Ayurvedic books, also stress the role of śukravaha srotas, the origin of which is in the vrsahana (testes) and sepha (penis). Suśruta describes that any trauma, obstruction or functional impairment of these structures results in such conditions as oligospermia, low motility, weak ejaculation, erectile dysfunction and infertility[5]. These interpretations are very much similar to the contemporary realization that the condition of the testicles, the ductal integrity and the best functioning of accessory glands are vital to the quality of semen[6,7].

2.2.1 Visible and Invisible Śukra

The division of śukra into visible and invisible which has been made by Ayurveda indicates a deep knowledge of reproductive physiology. Avyakta sukra is the subtle essence which pervades the whole body and helps in the vitality, energy, clarity of mind, enthusiasm and stability of mood. This very minute śukra is the one that is constantly fed through healthy eating, healthy habits and good mental activity. The disturbance of this aspect is expressed in the form of fatigue, hopelessness, the absence of sexual desire and psychological imbalances. Vyakta sukra, the expressed seminal fluid, is required in conception. This observable śukra is likened to the present-day semen which contains seminiferous tube spermatozoa and seminal plasma donated by the testes, epididymis, seminal vesicles, prostate, and other accessory glands[8]. The parameters that determine the quality of this śukra include the viscosity, colour, liquefaction, motility, and density among others.The idea thereby balances out the old and the new so that śukra may be taken as a subtle vital energy as well as a substance of reproduction[9].

2.2.2 Role of Dhātu Health

Ayurveda instructs that the dependence of sperm on any of the dhatus that precede it is wholly based on the quality of those before it. The homogeneity of metabolism (agni), the cleanliness of the channels of the body (srotas), and even the balance of the doṣas will always stand out to interfere with the formation of śukra. In case of weak digestion, there is a collection of the toxic metabolic by-products which block the srotas and block the flow of nutrients. This leads to the malformed formation of tissues, with śukra being the worst hit since it is the one to be at the end of the chain. Mental health is also an important factor- fear, stress, grief, anger and excessive worry is vitiating Vata and Pitta causing adverse effect on the sexual drive, ejaculation and semen quality. The contemporary science also recognizes stress, malnutrition, chronic disease, oxidative injury, and hormonal disturbance as the significant factors contribute to male infertility[10]

2.2.3 Śukravaha Srotas

Suśruta asserts that the śukravaha srotas are formed in the vrrshana (testes) and the sepha (penis). These are the means of conduction of the subtle and the manifested form of śukra. The hindrance, damage, or impairment of such paths will cause decreased seminal volume, low sperm count, aberrant motility, distorted viscosity, or defective sexual abilities. The abnormalities like Oligospermia, asthenospermia and teratospermia, reflect the classical concept of śukra doša where the amount, quality or functioning capability of srotas become blocked or disturbed due to the blockages of srotas. The patency of the srotas focuses on by Ayurveda perfectly coincides with contemporary focus on seminal vesicles, ejaculatory ducts, vas deferens, and accessory glands integrity.

2.3 Formation of Śukra Dhātu (Śukra Utpatti)

The formation of sperm is a highly advanced metabolic process that is referred to as dhatu parinama, whereby the nutrients converted to digested food gradually nourishes all the dhatu in the proper sequence. The seven dhatus are rasa, rakta, mamsa, medas, asthi, majja, and sukra which are grades of refinement with sukra being the refined and most powerful. The sperm (sukra) can only be formed after the six preceding dhatus have been nourished and they are devoid of any metabolic impurities. When this transformation is affected in any step, then the quality of śukra will be interfered with and hence infertility or lack of reproductive power.

The ayurvedic texts stress that the production of sperm is a continuous one and also premeditated by sexual stimulation. The invisible śukra gives nourishment to the body, but the visible kind of the same gathers in the reproductive organs to be ejaculated. Such similarity of classical and contemporary physiology is evidence of the wisdom of Ayurveda.

2.3.1 Dhātu Parinama (Sequential Transformation)

The rasa to śukra conversion is gradual where each dhatu would extract nourishment and continue to transfer its refined nature to the subsequent dhatu. This is a process of a subtle and profound metabolic chain. Any malfunction at one point or the other impacts all the following tissues so that śukra is especially susceptible to systemic inequalities. The state of śukra, thus, is an indicator of the quality of the formation of tissues in general and intra-organismal metabolism.

2.3.2 Role of Agni

The metabolic fire, Agni, is the focus of the purity of śukra. Under optimal functionality of jatharagni and dhathwagni, the nutrients are digested and absorbed, and pure essence is formed to each tissue. When agni is defective or disordered there is a formation of āma which blocks the channels, producing the result of thick, sticky, reduced in number, or malfunctioning of the śukra. It results in such clinical conditions like oligospermia, low motility, and abnormal morphology. The patterns of semen like increased viscosity, pus cell present, and abnormal-sized motility that is equivalent to the āma-induced śukra dohas in Ayurvedic literature[11]. Current clinical research also suggests that enhancing systemic metabolism and oxidative and metabolic stress reduction, e.g. by using Ashwagandha-based formulations, may be beneficial in terms of sperm count, motility, and seminal quality.[12, 13]

2.3.3 Influence of Doṣas

The doṣas have major roles in the development of śukra. Vata controls ejaculation, arousal, nerve, and the flow of semen the imbalance of which results in premature ejaculation, erectile dysfunction, decreased number of sperms, and dry or insufficient semen. Pitta controls transformation, coloration, and metabolic functions; when obstructed, it brings in burning issues, reduction of semen count and qualitative malformations. Kapha gives to the śukra the qualities of stability, viscosity and unctuousness; its imbalance causes too much thickness, too slow movement or blocking of the reproductive pathways. Such observations of classical literature are in close accordance with the diagnostic groups of oligospermia, asthenozoospermia, and teratozoospermia available in Ayurveda classics.

2.3.4 Factors Enhancing Śukra Formation

Śukra formation is greatly enhanced by nourishing, unctuous foods, emotional stability, adequate rest, healthy sexual practices, and the use of rasāyana and vajīkaraṇa herbs. A balanced daily routine and lifestyle strengthen metabolism, facilitate tissue nourishment, and maintain hormonal balance, thus promoting reproductive health.

2.3.5 Factors Impairing Śukra Formation

Conversely, factors such as overexertion, excessive indulgence, emotional disturbances, malnutrition, consumption of rukṣa or incompatible foods, substance abuse, and chronic illness impair śukra formation. The similar causes of male infertility, including nutritional deficiencies, systemic diseases, stress, environmental toxins, infections, and varicocele—highlighting how ancient and modern views converge.

2.4 Functions of Śukra Dhātu (Śukra Karma)

The roles of the śukra are much more than the reproduction. Its main function is the production of healthy progeny by way of fertilization, which is known as garbhotpada. In addition to this, śukra helps keep the body vital as it helps in enhancing strength, stamina, enthusiasm, and physical endurance. It adds to Ojas, the sublime material which produces immunity, balance of emotion and lifelong existence. The psychosomatic intensity of the effect of this dhatus is shown through the fact that Śukra grants the mind such qualities like joy, affection, creativity, and motivation.

The lubrication that is offered through śukra gives smooth operation of the reproductive channels and helps in ejaculation and sexual activity. These functions are very similar to the physiological functions of semen in the modern science which include nourishment and protection of spermatozoa, carrier of transportation, factors affecting conception success.

2.5 Properties of Śukra Dhātu (Śukra Guṇa)

The classical Ayurvedic texts assign such properties to the śukra: whiteness, sweetness, viscosity, unctuousness, heaviness, smoothness, and stability. These characteristics are incredibly close to the modern-day semen traits. Indicatively, the sweetness of śukra is associated with fructose which is largely released by the seminal vesicles. The viscous sticky quality is similar to the normal semen viscosity and its fluidity necessary to achieve healthy motility. Perfect density of the sperm is an indicator of its weight, whereas clear and smooth texture is an indicator of normal morphology and normal liquefaction patterns.

2.6 Ayurvedic Understanding of Reproductive Health

Ayurveda constantly reminds that a reproductive health is the manifestation of equilibrium of the whole body. It is necessary to nourish all dhatus since tissues like the previous ones cannot be healthy in case sperm becomes diseased. Psychological health is also of equal significance; stress, anxiety, anger, and grief all aggravate Vata and Pitta, and have a direct negative effect on the quality of śukra and sexual functioning.

A moderate way of life, right diet, follow-up of Dinacharya, good sleep, yoga, meditations, and regulated sexual behaviour (Brahmacarya in physiological sense) make šukra strong and reproductive vitality increased. Such principles resonate well with the current knowledge that the nutrition, exercise, oxidative stress, emotional state, endocrine regulation, and metabolic health are the factors that have a certain effect on fertility.

The Ayurveda recognizes the reproductive ability and the nourishment and energy of the body as a whole as

Sukra Dhatu, the finest and supreme of the tissues. Created by the successive refining of tissues, doṣhic balance relies on metabolic clarity, srotas clarity and emotional stability whereby the functions of the śukra extend very far beyond the production of sperm. It has classical characteristics that are similar to the contemporary semen parameters like the viscosity, motility, morphology, and vitality as evidenced in the literature. The physiology of śukra would thus be a solid starting point to the pathological conditions of male infertility and the development of effective Ayurvedic therapy regimes based on Rasāyana- Vajikaraṇa and Shodhana therapies.

References

1. Balwani, R. (2022). Shukra Dhatu-A Conceptual Study from Modern Perspective. Journal of Ayurveda and Integrated Medical Sciences, 7(4), 53-55.
2. Ca. Śārīrasthāna 2/4 Śukra as essence of all Dhātus
   शुक्रं तदस्य प्रवदन्ति धीरा यद्धीयते गर्भसमुद्भवाय।
   वाय्वग्निभूम्यब्गुणपादवत्तत् षड्भ्यो रसेभ्यः प्रभवश्च तस्य।।
3. Suśruta. (2003). Suśruta Saṃhitā (K. Sharma, Trans.). Chaukhambha Visvabharati.
   Su. Sūtrasthāna 15/5 — Functions of Śukra
   शुक्रं धैर्यं च्यवनं प्रीतिं देहबलं हर्षं बीजार्थं च।
4. Chouhan, B. S., Rajput, S. S., Dwivedi, R., & Singh, A. K. (2018). A review on ayurveda perspective and therapeutic consideration of oligozoospermia. Journal of Drug Delivery & Therapeutics
5. Sabnis, S. S., & Hiremath, V. (2022). Ayurvedic management of Ksheena Shukra-A Case Study. Journal of Ayurveda and Integrated Medical Sciences, 7(1), 406-410.
6. Ca. Vimānasthāna 5/8 Roots of Śukravaha Srotas
   शक्रवाहानां स्रोतसां वृषणौ मूलं शेफश्च।

7. Su. Śārīrasthāna 9/14 — Origin of Śukravaha Srotas
शुक्रवहे द्वे तयोर्मूलं स्तनौ वृषणौ च।

8. Nasimi Doost Azgomi, R., Zomorrodi, A., Nazemyieh, H., Fazljou, S. M. B., Sadeghi Bazargani, H., Nejatbakhsh, F. & Ahmadi AsrBadr, Y. (2018). Effects of Withania somnifera on reproductive system: a systematic review of the available evidence. BioMed research international, 2018(1), 4076430.

9. Su. Śārīrasthāna 3/3 — Saumya nature of Śukra
सौम्यं शुक्रमार्तवमाग्नेयमितरेषामप्यत्र भूतानां
सान्निध्यमस्त्यणुना विशेषेण परस्परोपकारात्॥

10. Ca. Cikitsāsthāna 30/154–157 — Characteristics of kṣīṇa-śukra / klaibya
सङ्कल्पप्रवणो नित्यं प्रियां वश्यामपि स्त्रियम्।
न याति लिङ्गशैथिल्यात् कदाचिद्याति वा यदि॥
श्वासार्तः स्विन्नगात्रश्च मोघसङ्कल्पचेष्टितः।
म्लानशिश्नश्च निर्बीजः स्यादेतत् क्लैब्यलक्षणम्॥

11. Ambiye, V. R., Langade, D., Dongre, S., Aptikar, P., Kulkarni, M., & Dongre, A. (2013). Clinical evaluation of the spermatogenic activity of the root extract of Ashwagandha (Withania somnifera) in oligospermic males: a pilot study. Evidence-Based Complementary and Alternative Medicine, 2013(1), 571420.

12. A.H. Sūtrasthāna 7/61–67 — Behavioral causes of Dhātu-kṣaya / Śukra-kṣaya
अतियोगाच्चेष्टायाः श्रमात् पानान्नविहारतः।
व्यासङ्गादग्निनाशाच्च वायुः प्रकोपमृच्छति॥
ततो धातून् प्रकर्षेण शोषयत्यग्निना यथा।

13. Maria, Y. P. T., & de Araujo Camilla, O. D. (2019). Effect of Withania somnifera in the treatment of male infertility: a literature review. Journal of Medicinal Plants Research, 13(18), 473-479.

Chapter - 3

Etiology and Classification of Male Infertility

3.1 Introduction to Male Infertility

Male infertility has been embraced as a multifactorial, multicomponent, multifaceted ailment that manifests as a complication of a complex interaction of physiological, metabolic, psychological, as well as environmental factors. Rather than being confined to issues regarding the reproductive organs per se, male infertility is a broad derailment of the overall status of the state of health, hormonal processes, food provision to the tissues and genetic integrity. The modern andrologic research has included an extensive list of contributory factors that includes hormonal disturbances, impaired spermatogenesis, varicocele, infections, oxidative stress, environmental toxins, lifestyle behaviors[1] and idiopathic malfunctions that have potential to alter the sperm concentration, motility, morphology and reproductive potential. This complexity aids in pointing out the fact that fertility in males is not a biological process that happens in isolation but is an explanatory indicator of overall physical and metabolic health[2].

Ayurveda provides a rather comprehensive but different view of male infertility, which is perceived as a condition that is based on the disruptions of doṣha, disrupted tissue metabolism (dhātu parinama), impaired digestive fire (agni), blockage or weakness of reproductive channels (śukravaha srotas), and depletion or vitiation of śukra dhatu. Where modern science considers infertility in terms of quantifiable factors, e.g., the levels of hormones, semen analysis and testicular activity, Ayurveda views the issue in terms of qualitative measurements of vitality, nutrition, circulation and harmoniousness of mind and body. Despite the differences in the frameworks, the two are astonishingly complementary: they both recognize how reproductive health is closely dependent on the lifestyle, diet, stress, systemic diseases, metabolic dysfunction and environmental exposures[3].

In such a way, male infertility can be discussed as a mutual point of intersection between contemporary biomedical knowledge and Ayurvedic knowledge. This integrative conceptual base is required to comprehend the accurate etiological pathways of infertility as well as to develop holistic and effective therapeutic interventions[4], something that will be discussed in the ensuing parts of this chapter.

3.2 Modern Etiology of Male Infertility

Modern andrology acknowledges male infertility as an illness which is caused by a very broad range of biological, hormonal, environmental and lifestyle-based influences which disrupt the spermiogenesis, maturation, transportation and activity. These causes are usually grouped into pre-testicular, testicular and post-testicular causes, which reveal the complexity of the male reproductive system and several levels where the damage may be introduced.

Most common cause of infertility in males, which is known as spermatogenic failure, is an impaired functionality of the testes that influence the manufacture of spermatozoa. Varicocele, undescended testes, genetic anomalies, testicular trauma, orchitis, exposure to gonadotropins and degenerative testicular conditions are primary testicular factors. These include, diminished sperm concentration, motor and degenerated morphology as a result of disruption of Sertoli and Leydig cell functionality, oxidative stress, elevated scrotal temperature and disruption of microcirculation within the testes.[5]

Those that pre-testicular relate with hypothalamic pituitary gonadal axis abnormalities. The FSH, LH and testosterone secretion are impaired by conditions like hypogonadotropic hypogonadism, pituitary adenomas, thyroid disorders, hyperprolactinaemia and systemic endocrine disturbances which are all necessary in the regulation of spermatogenesis. Dysregulation of hormones may be observed in the form of low sperm count, reduced volume of semen, low motility of semen and distorted seminal fluid properties.

The post-testicular aetiologies are caused by structural or functional disruptions in the passage of the sperm along the reproductive tract. The failure of the flow of sperm is due to obstruction of the epididymis, vas deferens or ejaculatory ducts, which are congenital, infectious, inflammatory or iatrogenic. The functional disorders which include retrograde ejaculation, anejaculation and ejaculatory dysfunction also add to infertility by hindering the transmission of sperm during sexual activity. The conditions usually manifest through the low semen volume, slow semen liquefaction, change in viscosity or absence of sperm in ejaculate.

The lifestyle and environmental factors are also found to have a considerable impact in modern research. Smoking and the excessive use of alcohol, obesity, chronic stress, exposure to heat, sedentary activities, environmental toxins, endocrine disruptors and recreational drugs have adverse effects on sperm functioning. These are aspects that contribute to oxidative stress, fragmentation of DNA, morphological abnormalities and decreased motility, all of which seriously impair the potential to reproduce.[6]

Even with the current improvement in diagnostic methods, a significant number of men can be termed as being of idiopathic infertility whereby seminal parameters are abnormal and no definite aetiology is identified. This indicates the shortcoming of knowledge regarding the delicate metabolic, genetic, epigenetic and environmental factors that can influence reproductive functioning. The shortcomings of existing diagnostics techniques suggest the importance of more systemic and comprehensive approaches to male infertility, leading to integrative models that will unite modern and traditional medical views upon the matter.

3.3 Ayurvedic Etiology of Male Infertility (Bīja Duṣṭi / Kṣīṇa Śukra / Klaibya)

Ayurveda presents a multi-dimensional and holistic approach to the concept of male infertility that is mainly explained with the help of the notions of bija duṣti, ksina sukra and klaibya. In comparison to the reductionist biomedical approach, Ayurveda is characterized by fertility being a result of the smooth functioning of, agni, dhatus and srotases. When these principles are disturbed, they may have an effect of disrupting the formation, quality or ability of sperm in the body, thus leading to infertility. The classical Ayurvedic texts have explicit explanations about how variations in the physiological equilibrium of the body, starting with the digestive system and emotional strains to the lodging of channels and the draining of the system, may result in a lack of reproductive ability in men.

3.3.1 Doṣha-Based Etiology

In Ayurveda, the doṣhas Vata, Pitta and Kapha are a major cause of healthy and unhealthy maintenance of the male reproductive system. Vata dosha, especially when exaggerated, induces the depletion of the sukra dhatu, resulting in the reduced quantity of sperms, ejaculation disorders and dhatu-kshaya. The dry and unpredictable nature of vata interferes with the nutrients that the sperm needs to be nourished to form normal sperms, usually leading to low libido, premature ejaculation or impotence.

The vitiation of the qualitative aspects of śukra is caused by pitta doṣa. The excess Pitta produces heat which can cause discoloration, burning sensations, decrease in the volume of semen and as well as a decline in the sperm morphology. These qualitative flaws reflect the contemporary knowledge of the oxidative stress and heat damage of sperm.[7]

When kapha doṣha gets aggravated, it enhances the weight, viscosity and thickness of semen, which slows down sperm motions and prevents flowing. The unctuous and stabilizing qualities of kapha are in excess thus making the seminal fluid too thick and sticky thus preventing the smooth movement of the spermatozoa and their proper functioning.

3.3.2 Srotoduṣṭi (Channel Pathology)

Ayurveda blames a lot of reproductive disorders to srotoduṣhti or pathology of the bodily channels especially srotas of the shukra. Sanga, or blockage in these pathways, is what is today referred to as obstructive azoospermia or obstruction of the ejaculatory ducts. The excessive or abnormal flow of reproductive fluids, called atipravrtti, can take the form of premature ejaculation or the availability of thin, watery semen that is not very vigorous.

Siria-granthi is termed as varicosity or nodular swellings in the channels and it is similar to a clinical condition of varicocele which causes defective testicular temperature and sperm production. Vimarga gamana, the misdirected flow, describes such things as retrograde ejaculation, in which semen does not shoot out of the urethra but instead into the urinary bladder.[8]

3.3.3 Avarana (Occlusion-Type Pathology)

The term āvarana nan is the concept of the blocking or occlusion of a physiological force by a second one. Vata-avarana is vital in the infertility of men. As Vata is blocked by other doṣhas or tissues, the usual process of ejaculation, erecting and moving of semen is interfered with. This can lead to ejaculatory dysfunction, poor erection, lack of libido or sexual dysfunction.

On the same note, when Vata is obstructed by Kapha or medas, thick and immobile semen may result with low motility. Excess Kapha blocks channels, causes heaviness, which causes difficulty of movement of sperm and unhealthy seminal fluid, similar to such conditions as severe asthenozoospermia.[9]

3.3.4 Agnimandya and Āma

One major etiological Ayurvedic term is agnimandya or reduced digestive and metabolic fire. The agni becomes impaired and develops āma, which is the toxic and undigested metabolic by-product that circulates within the body and interferes with the formation of the tissues. The contamination of the dhatus by āma leads to poor nourishment of the spermatozoa in the form of immature, weak, or morphologically deformed spermatozoa.

Moreover, the āma blocks the srotas of sukra, which is one of the causes of viscosity, decreased liquefaction and inflammatory reactions. This is associated with current situations like leukocytospermia, inflammatory semen abnormality and oxidative stress induced sperm malfunction.

3.3.5 Manasika Nidāna (Psychological Factors)

Ayurveda recognizes the immense effects of psychological factors on the reproductive health of males. Vata dosha is worsening by such emotional states as stress, anxiety, fear, grief and depression, which interfere with the normal functioning of the mind body axis. This may result in low libido, lack of erection, premature ejaculation and low quality of sperm. Such classical descriptions coincide well with the current scientific discoveries that promote elevation of cortisol, inflict oxidative effects, disturb hormonal equilibrium and positively contribute to infertility.

Ayurveda introduces the male infertility as the outcome of the systemic imbalance in the form of doṣhas, the malfunctioning of metabolism, the blocked reproductive channels and the broken emotional balance. This integrative etiological model is more insightful than contemporary information as it provides a more profound interpretation of delicate physiological and psychosomatic mechanisms that influence male fertility.

3.4 The Four Essential Fertility Factors in Ayurveda

Conception according to Ayurveda is an undertaking that is highly coordinated and this functioning is dependent on four fundamental aspects, and it is referred to as Rtu, Kshetra, Ambu and Bija. It is founded on Ayurvedic classical embryology and may be applied to describe the circumstances of successful reproduction and the fragile balance of physiological preparedness, environmental conditions, tissue nutrition and gametogenic quality. These concepts of Ayurveda can be compared in the context of contemporary reproductive science, to the contemporary understanding of the hormonal balance, the integrity of the anatomy, the seminal plasma structure and the genetics of spermic cells. They offer a massive convergence of male fertility.

3.4.1 Ṛtu (Optimal Timing / Fertile Period / Internal Rhythms)

Ṛtu refers to the ideal timing and physiological preparedness required for conception. Despite the common understanding of this term as the fertility cycle in women, this would be applied to the larger term of natural rhythms, seasonal forces and the general reproductive healthiness of both partners. For the male, Ṛtu includes hormonal stability, optimal sexual function, and general wellbeing that support healthy spermatogenesis.

In modern understanding, Rtu is associated with getting the hormonal cycles in harmony, the time of the intercourse during the fertile period, and the state of the body that promotes optimal sperm motility and viability. It is a testament to the relevance of endocrine homeostasis, stress control and circadian rhythm- aspects which have a profound effect on sperm production and fertility.

3.4.2 Kṣhetra (Healthy Reproductive Field)

Kṣhetra denotes the reproductive field or anatomical foundation required for conception. In men it encompasses the structure and good functioning of the testes (vṛṣaṇa), penis (śepha), epididymis, prostate, seminal vesicles and the whole system of reproductive ducts. Healthy Kṣhetra ensures the appropriate formation, maturation, storage and delivery of sperm.

In Modern, this is equivalent to anatomical patency, accessory gland functioning and a clear passage of sperm along the vas deferens and ejaculatory ducts. Structural abnormalities, inflammation, infection or congenital defects influence this field leading to obstructive infertility, ejaculatory dysfunction or poor seminal plasma quality. Therefore, the Ayurvedic concept of Kshetra offers a whole body anatomical model that is directly related to contemporary reproductive anatomy.

3.4.3 Ambu (Nutritional Fluid / Supportive Milieu)

Ambu represents the nutritional and biochemical environment necessary for the nourishment and vitality of *śukra dhātu*. It includes the essence of rasa *dhātu* and the fluids that provide sustenance to all bodily tissues. In the context of male fertility, Ambu is responsible for maintaining the supportive milieu that allows for healthy sperm formation and maturation.

Ambu is now recognized by modern correlations as being wholly composed of seminal plasma that contains fructose, citric acid, minerals, proteins, enzymes, hormones and antioxidants necessary to maintain sperm viability and motility. Factors including pH equilibrium, osmolarity, viscosity and nutrient provision assume very important roles in the means of ensuring optimality of functionality of the spermatozoa. The impairment of this seminal environment through infections, oxidative stress or metabolic imbalance directly influences sperm health, which explains the great applicability of Ambu to the modern field of reproductive biology.

3.4.4 Bīja (Gamete Quality / Genetic Integrity)

The gametophyte or the seed of life is called Bijas. The sperm (śuddha bīja) is supposed to be alive, structurally sound, of appropriate morphology and capable of producing healthy offspring as per Ayurveda. Any pollution or dysfunction in Bijas causes the compromised fertility or birth defect or suboptimal reproductive performance.

The sperm cell and its genetic wholeness is called Bijas in modern science. This is stability of chromatin, index of fragmentation of DNA, normal morphology, no motility and viability to fertilize ovum. The defects of these parameters are caused by oxidative stress, hereditary mutations, varicocele, environmental toxins or poor lifestyle and reduce fertility potential. Consequently, the concept of Bijas would be an apt comparison to the modern-day assessment of sperm DNA quality, which is genetic fitness and efficiency.

The Ayurvedic fertility factors—Ṛtu, Kṣhetra, Ambu and Bīja—form an elegant and holistic framework that aligns strongly with modern reproductive science. All these are different aspects of fertility that continue to play some clinical part in the contemporary world, which offers a point of reference between the previous and the novel knowledge on male reproductive health.

3.5 Classification of Male Infertility

Male infertility classification gives a fundamental structure to the study of the varied clinical manifestations and pathogenesis that disrupt the reproductive performance. Communities of both modern and Ayurvedic systems have taken a complementary stance, and can assist clinicians to determine the nature of a particular seminal dysfunction and formulate therapeutic approaches. Modern andrology categorizes infertility based on semen analysis, hormonal patterns and anatomical considerations, whereas Ayurveda classifies infertility through qualitative assessments of śukra dhātu, doṣha involvement and reproductive channel pathology. All these systems give an overall foundation to diagnosis and treatment of male infertility.

3.5.1 Modern Classification

The male infertility of the modern reproductive medicine is mainly categorized based on the parameters of semen as per the standardized laboratory criteria. Oligozoospermia occurs due to decreased level of sperm density and is further divided into mild, moderate and severe oligozoospermia based on the extent of decreased level. Asthenozoospermia is characterized by low sperm motility and it is further classified into grades of progressive, non-progressive and immotile sperms. The changes in the motility grades indicate disruptions in energy metabolism, tail structure or seminal environment.

Teratozoospermia is the abnormal morphology of sperm in which a considerable percentage of sperm have morphological defects in head, midpiece or tail. Such morphological defects impair the fertilization of an ovum by a sperm. A low count of sperm, poor motility and abnormal morphology exist in most men together, creating the category of Oligoasthenoteratozoospermia (OATS) - which is a common and, in many cases, a hard-to-treat manifestation.

In more severe forms, azoospermia is a diagnosis of the absence of spermatozoa in the ejaculate. This can be obstructive which is caused by obstructions of the reproductive ducts or non-obstructive which shows testicular failure in the production of sperm. Necrozoospermia, which occurs when there is immotile but non-viable sperm, and aspermia, which is the absence of ejaculate despite orgasm, are other types of categories of reproductive dysfunction.

This new classification scheme assists clinicians in determining particular patterns of seminal impairment and direct selective diagnostic assessment of the underlying hormonal, genetic or anatomic aberration.

3.5.2 Ayurvedic Classification

Ayurveda classifies male infertility as qualitative and functional indicators of shukra dhatu whose quantity, quality and reproductive capacity can be abnormal across a broad range. The nearest classical analogue of oligospermia is kšīṇa śukra, which is decreased semen volume, low count of sperm or poor quality semen that is inadequately competent to fertilize the egg. In addition to the quantity, Ayurveda defines qualitative defects, pita śukra, kṛshna śukra, guru śukra and asma śukra, a defect of each defect in color, consistency, density or subtlety of the seminal fluid. These differences are associated with morphological or functional flaws that have been identified in contemporary seminal diagnosis.

The disorders like śukra-kṣhaya (the loss of the reproductive tissue), śukra- āvarana (the blockage or obstruction to the proper ejaculation or movement of the semen) and śukra-duṣti (pollution or impairment of the semen) provide an added insight into the pathological alterations in the reproductive physiology. These categories are a wide spectrum of dysfunctions such as poor motility, abnormal viscosity, inflammatory alterations as well as the impaired reproductive potency.[10]

Ayurveda refers to the term klaibya as a broad term to cover erectile dysfunction, ejaculatory problems and functional infertility. It points out the combined sexual, psychological and physical aspects of male reproductive health. The inability to generate healthy offspring despite normal sexual contact is termed in another classical term apatyakshamat, the inability to give birth to healthy offspring after attempting typical sexual activity- both genetic and functional impairment of reproductive ability.

Ayurvedic classification therefore provides a multidimensional approach to the male infertility, which is textured, all the slightest abnormalities in the quality of tissues, systemic harmony and reproductive activity and provides highly helpful information about personal approach to treatment.

3.6 Integrative Ayurvedic–Modern Correlation

The Ayurvedic and the modern biomedical approaches to male infertility, despite being based on different epistemological approaches, overlap in many ways when they are considered in the light of common physiological and pathological principles. Ayurveda describes infertility as an outcome of disturbances in doṣhas, impaired srotas, weakened agni, formation of āma and defects in bīja and ambu. Contemporary science, in turn, singles out endocrine disruption, oxidative stress, anatomical blockage, inflammation and damaged sperm DNA integrity as key factors that cause male infertility. This integrative knowledge demonstrates that the two systems are highly compatible and can be used to provide important insights in the diagnosis and management of the whole system.

Ayurveda attributes many reproductive disturbances to doṣha vitiation, which closely parallels hormonal dysregulation, oxidative damage and abnormalities in sperm production described in modern andrology. Vata vitiation interferes with semen motility and expulsion, which is similar to ejaculatory dysfunction and low sperm motility. Pitta aggravation produces too much heat, which is associated with oxidative stress, defective sperm morphology, and DNA damage. Overabundance of kapha causes heaviness, slowness and viscosity of semen, which are similar to low motility and structural defects of semen analysis. Thus, the Ayurvedic model of doṣha imbalance aligns closely with endocrine, metabolic and cellular factors recognized in contemporary reproductive medicine.

The Ayurvedic theory of srotoduṣhti, or pathology of body channels, gives additional areas of correspondence. Conditions like sanga (obstruction) are similar to obstructive azoospermia or ejaculatory duct blockage and sira-granthi (varicosities) is similar to varicocele, which is one of the major causes of impaired spermatogenesis in contemporary medicine. The functional abnormalities, such as retrograde ejaculation, may be considered in the perspective of vimarga gamana (misdirection of flow). This shows such an anatomical and functional correspondence between ancient accounts of srotas impairment and current typologies of obstructive and non-obstructive infertility.

The development of āma as a result of agni impairment is similar to inflammatory and infectious diseases of the male reproductive tract. Ayurveda āma blocks the srotas of the semen. Increased viscosity, delayed liquefaction, abnormal pH and the presence of pus cells are similar manifestations of androgens identified by modern andrology as indicative of inflammation, oxidative stress and defective seminal plasma composition. Both models highlight the negative impact of the metabolic toxins or inflammatory by-products on the sperm vitality and functionality.

Ayurveda's understanding of Bīja duṣṭi, or defects in the reproductive seed, correlates strongly with modern insights into sperm DNA fragmentation, chromatin instability, structural defects and genetic abnormalities. Similar to Ayurveda, which defines corrupted bīja as one that cannot generate healthy offspring, the current research indicates that DNA damage and chromosomal aberrations are the leading causes of infertility, frequent pregnancy loss and low assisted reproductive success.

The Ayurvedic principle of Ambu, the nourishing fluid that makes the tissues alive, is quite similar to the nourishing fluid in contemporary science, the seminal plasma. Seminal plasma is a source of nutrients, antioxidants, optimum pH and biochemical conditions needed in sperm motility and fertilization. Ambu deficiency is associated with low seminal plasma composition, micronutrient deficiencies, low antioxidant capacity and impaired biochemical milieu- which are conditions that severely impair sperm functioning.

All these integrative correlations show that Ayurveda and modern andrology have quite different names, but the reported pathogenic mechanisms are very similar. These intersections will enable us to learn more about male infertility and to establish holistic, synergistic treatment methods that take into account both systemic and reproductive health.

Male infertility is a complex multifactorial disease, which is shaped by complex physiological, metabolic, anatomic and psychological interplay. Modern andrology has attributed the factors to a wide range of causes that cause the abnormalities, including hormonal disturbances, spermatogenesis defects, anatomical obstructions, lifestyle factors and oxidative stress, leading to oligozoospermia, asthenozoospermia, teratozoo spermia, azoospermia and all of the previously mentioned factors. Such classes can be seen as measurable changes in sperm counts, motility, morphology and seminal quality.

Ayurveda offers a systemic viewpoint that sees male infertility in terms of Kshīna sukra, Bijadushti and Klaibya. It is the disturbances of doṣhas, the impairment of agni, the development of ama, sroto dushti and the violation of the integrity of the dhatu parinama till śukra are the basis of Ayurvedic aetiology. The classical model also demonstrates the importance of four main fertility factors i.e. Rtu, Ksetra, Ambu and Bija, which are the main physiological aspects of the modern reproductive concepts of hormonal synchronization, anatomical wellbeing, biochemical background and gametical integrity.

On closer look, there exist such impressive analogy between Ayurvedic and modern etiopathology. Doṣha vitiation reflects hormonal and metabolic pathology, Srotoduṣthi is anatomical obstruction and ejaculatory dysfunction, āma is inflammation, altered viscosity and oxidative injury, Bijadusti is sperm DNA and chromatin defects, and Ambu lacks are comparable to poor seminal plasma composition and micronutrient deficiency. These integrative observations show how Ayurvedic knowledge is rich and can be applied to the current science of reproduction.

In general, Chapter 3 provides a single framework of male infertility through the reconciliation of classical Ayurvedic theories with contemporary biomedical categories. This integrative methodology forms the basis of developing holistic diagnostic plans and treatment plans, which will be discussed in later chapters.

References

1. Durairajanayagam, D. (2018). Lifestyle causes of male infertility. Arab journal of urology, 16(1), 10-20.

2. Levine, H., Jørgensen, N., Martino-Andrade, A., Mendiola, J., Weksler-Derri, D., Mindlis, I., & Swan, S. H. (2017). Temporal trends in sperm count: a systematic review and meta-regression analysis. Human reproduction update, 23(6), 646-659.

3. Ca. Śārīrasthāna 2/4 — Śukra as essence of all Dhātus
शुक्रं तदस्य प्रवदन्ति धीरा यद्धीयते गर्भसमुद्भवाय।
वाय्वग्निभूम्यब्गुणपादवत्तत् षड्भ्यो रसेभ्यः प्रभवश्च तस्य॥

4. Dissanayake, D. M. I. H., et al. (2019). Male infertility problem: A contemporary review. Gender & the Genome.

5. Liang, Y., Huang, J., Zhao, Q., Mo, H., Su, Z., Feng, S., ... & Ruan, X. (2025). Global, regional, and national prevalence and trends of infertility among individuals of reproductive age (15–49 years) from 1990 to 2021, with projections to 2040. Human Reproduction, 40(3), 529-544.

6. Huang, B., Wang, Z., Kong, Y., Jin, M., & Ma, L. (2023). Global, regional and national burden of male infertility in 204 countries and territories between 1990 and 2019: an analysis of global burden of disease study. BMC Public Health, 23(1), 2195.

7. Ca. Cikitsāsthāna 30/154–157 — Kṣīṇa-śukra / Klaibya lakṣaṇa
सङ्कल्पप्रवणो नित्यं प्रियां वश्यामपि स्त्रियम्।
न याति लिङ्गशैथिल्यात् कदाचिद्याति वा यदि॥
श्वासार्तः स्विन्नगात्रश्च मोघसङ्कल्पचेष्टितः।

8. Su. Śārīrasthāna 9/14 — Mūla of Śukravaha Srotas
शुक्रवहे द्वे तयोर्मूलं स्तनौ वृषणौ च।

9. A.H. Sūtrasthāna 12/9 — Apāna Vāyu & reproductive function
अपानोऽपानगः श्रोणिबस्तिमेढ्रोरुगोचरः।
शुक्रार्तवशकृन्मूत्रगर्भनिष्क्रमणक्रियः॥

10. Su. Sūtrasthāna 2/11 — Physical properties of Śukra
स्फटिकाभं द्रवं स्निग्धं मधुरं मधुगन्धि च।

Chapter - 4

Clinical Features and Diagnosis

Male infertility manifests as a constellation of reproductive, physical and psychological disturbances that reflect deeper systemic imbalances. While modern biomedicine defines male infertility through quantifiable parameters such as sperm count, motility and morphology, Ayurveda interprets it as a disturbance of *śukra dhātu, dohṣa, Agni, srotas* and overall vitality. The convergence of both systems reveals a comprehensive clinical picture in which reproductive dysfunction is understood not merely as a localized disease of the testes or seminal fluid but as the outcome of complex physiological, metabolic, emotional and environmental factors. This chapter provides an integrated overview of the classical Ayurvedic symptoms of male infertility along with contemporary diagnostic approaches, offering a unified framework for understanding and evaluating this multifactorial condition.

4.1 Classical Ayurvedic Clinical Features

Ayurveda describes male infertility through clinically recognizable categories such as *Klaibya, Kṣīṇa Śukra* and *Apraja.* These categories encompass sexual dysfunction, depleted reproductive potential and impaired gamete vitality, all of which align strongly with patterns seen in modern andrology.[1,2,3]

4.1.1 Klaibya

Klaibya is a broad term encompassing conditions in which the male is unable to perform sexual intercourse satisfactorily or produce healthy offspring. It includes disturbances in erection, ejaculation, libido and sexual vigour, all of which are governed largely by *Vāta doṣa*. When Vāta becomes aggravated—due to stress, anxiety, excessive exertion, poor diet or chronic illness—it disrupts neuromuscular and vascular mechanisms essential for erection and ejaculation. Patients may present with erectile weakness, premature ejaculation, lack of confidence, weak ejaculation force, decreased sexual desire and performance anxiety. Ayurveda identifies multiple subtypes of *Klaibya* (Vātaja, Pittaja, Kaphaja, Sannipātaja), each corresponding to specific patterns of dysfunction, such as burning sensations (Pitta), excessive heaviness and sluggishness (Kapha), or loss of vigour due to depletion.[4]

4.1.2 Kṣīṇa Śukra

Kṣīṇa Śukra refers to the depletion or deterioration of *śukra dhātu*, resulting in poor quality and insufficient quantity of semen. Clinically, it manifests as scanty, thin, watery, discoloured or non-viscous semen, often accompanied by reduced libido, mental fatigue, weakness after coitus and diminished reproductive vitality. Ayurveda attributes this condition to weak Agni, poor nourishment of the dhātus, chronic illness, emotional strain or obstruction of reproductive channels.[5]. In modern terms, this maps closely to oligospermia, low semen volume, poor motility, altered viscosity and morphological defects, highlighting a clear overlap between traditional and contemporary clinical observations.[6]

4.1.3 Apraja

Apraja denotes infertility or the inability to produce progeny despite engaging in regular, unprotected sexual activity. The condition may arise from factors affecting the *bīja* (sperm quality), *Ambu* (nutritional milieu), *kṣetra* (reproductive organs) or systemic imbalances in *doṣas* and *srotas*. Patients may exhibit normal sexual desire and performance but fail to achieve conception due to underlying defects in sperm vitality, hormonal imbalance, poor seminal environment or genetic abnormalities. Ayurveda emphasizes that healthy progeny can be conceived only when *ṛtu, kṣetra, Ambu,* and *bīja* are all optimal—underscoring a comprehensive, multidimensional understanding of male fertility.

4.2 Additional Ayurvedic Indicators

In addition to these classical categories, Ayurveda recognizes several subtle indicators of male reproductive dysfunction. Disturbed *Agni* leads to *Ama* accumulation, which obstructs *śukravaha srotas* and degrades sperm quality. *Avarana* (occlusion of Vāta by Kapha or Medas) causes ejaculatory difficulty, thick semen and sluggish motility. Mental disturbances such as worry, fear, grief and depression vitiate Vāta and directly impair sexual desire and reproductive performance.[7] Ayurveda also analyses the patient's digestion, sleep, vitality, complexion and emotional health—all critical determinants of *śukra* formation.[8]

4.3 Contemporary Clinical Features

Modern medicine recognizes male infertility largely through abnormalities in semen parameters, hormonal imbalances, sexual dysfunction and structural defects in the reproductive tract.[9]

4.3.1 Sexual and Reproductive Symptoms

Men may report decreased libido, erectile dysfunction, premature ejaculation, weak ejaculation, delayed ejaculation or anejaculation. Changes in semen volume, consistency, smell or colour are commonly observed. Pain during ejaculation or a history of infections, surgeries or trauma may accompany reproductive difficulty.[10]

4.3.2 Systemic Indicators

Male infertility is often associated with broader systemic symptoms such as reduced muscle mass, fatigue, mood changes, gynecomastia or metabolic conditions like obesity and diabetes. These symptoms suggest hormonal decline, endocrine disturbances or chronic illness, all of which directly affect spermatogenesis.

4.4 Modern Diagnostic Framework

Modern diagnosis relies on objective assessment tools that evaluate semen quality, hormonal balance, anatomical integrity and cellular health of sperm.[11]

4.4.1 Semen Analysis (WHO Standard Parameters)

Semen analysis is the cornerstone of male infertility evaluation. It measures:

- Sperm concentration
- Total sperm count
- Motility (progressive, non-progressive, immotile)
- Morphology
- Semen volume
- Viscosity
- Liquefaction time
- pH and appearance

Abnormalities such as oligozoospermia, asthenozoospermia, teratozoospermia, OATS, azoospermia, necrozoospermia and aspermia form the basis of clinical diagnosis and guide further evaluation.

Baseline semen analysis from clinical observations showed consistent abnormalities across all cases, including low sperm concentration (11–14 million/mL), severely delayed liquefaction times exceeding 90 minutes to 2 hours, and markedly reduced motility (15–22%). These diagnostic findings align closely with modern classifications such as oligozoospermia, asthenozoospermia and oligo-asthenozoospermia.

From an Ayurvedic perspective, these patterns correspond to *Kṣīṇa Śukra, Śukra Duṣṭi,* Kapha-Meda *Āvaraṇa,* and *Srotorodha* affecting the *śukravaha srotas.* The following table summarizes the diagnostic features observed in three documented cases.

Table 1: Baseline Semen Analysis of Three Clinical Cases

Parameter	Case 1	Case 2	Case 3
Semen Volume (mL)	1.5 mL	2.0 mL	1.8 mL
Liquefaction Time	> 2 hours (severely delayed)	> 90 minutes (delayed)	> 2 hours (severely delayed)
Sperm Concentration	14 million/mL	11 million/mL	13 million/mL
Sperm Motility	20%	15%	22%

Diagnostic Pattern	Oligospermia + Asthenozoospermia + Delayed Liquefaction	Moderate Oligospermia + Severe Asthenozoospermia + High Viscosity	Oligo-Asthenozoospermia + High Viscosity + Severe Liquefaction Delay
Ayurvedic Interpretation	Kṣīṇa Śukra, Vāta–Kapha imbalance	Śukra Duṣṭi, Kapha-Meda Āvaraṇa	Kṣīṇa Śukra + Kapha Āvaraṇa + Srotorodha

4.4.2 Hormonal Profile

Endocrine evaluation assesses FSH, LH, testosterone, prolactin and thyroid hormones to identify pre-testicular causes such as hypogonadism, pituitary dysfunction or metabolic disorders that impact spermatogenesis.

4.4.3 Imaging and Structural Assessment

Scrotal ultrasonography detects varicocele, tumours or structural anomalies. Doppler studies evaluate vascular flow, while transrectal ultrasound helps identify ejaculatory duct obstruction or seminal vesicle abnormalities.

4.4.4 Advanced Diagnostic Tools

More specialized investigations include:

- Sperm DNA fragmentation tests
- Oxidative stress markers
- Genetic testing (karyotyping, Y-chromosome microdeletions)
- Tests for antisperm antibodies
- Microbiological analysis for infections

These modern assessments help uncover hidden or subtle aetiologies that may not manifest in routine semen analysis.

4.5 Integrative Diagnostic Correlation

The convergence between Ayurvedic and modern diagnostics reveals striking parallels:

- *Kṣīṇa Śukra* corresponds to low sperm count, poor seminal viscosity and motility defects.
- *Klaibya* parallels erectile dysfunction, premature ejaculation and psychosexual disturbances.
- *Śukra duṣṭi* reflects abnormal morphology, viscosity, odor or liquefaction patterns.
- *Ama* formation parallels inflammatory semen profiles, presence of leukocytes and altered biochemical properties.
- *Srotodushti* matches obstructive pathologies such as ejaculatory duct blockage or vas deferens obstruction.
- Disturbed *Agni* and *doṣa* imbalance align with endocrine dysfunction, metabolic disorders and oxidative stress.
- Defective *bīja* corresponds directly to DNA fragmentation, chromatin instability and genetic anomalies.

This integrative approach enriches diagnostic precision by combining Ayurvedic insights into systemic imbalance with modern laboratory-based evaluations.

4.6 Summary

Clinical evaluation of male infertility requires a broad perspective that includes both classical Ayurvedic insights and modern investigative techniques. Ayurveda identifies symptomatic patterns reflecting disturbances in *doṣhas, dhātu* metabolism, emotional wellbeing and reproductive vitality. Modern diagnostics provide measurable parameters that define semen quality, hormonal balance and structural integrity. Together, these systems create a comprehensive diagnostic framework that not only identifies the root causes of infertility but also lays the foundation for personalized, holistic and effective treatment strategies.

References

1. Leaver, R. B. (2016). Male infertility: an overview of causes and treatment options. British Journal of Nursing, 25(18), S35-S40.

2. Vāgbhaṭa. (2007). Aṣṭāṅga Saṃgraha (K. R. Srikantha Murthy, Trans.). Chaukhambha Orientalia.

(a) A.S. Uttarasthāna 40/44 — Qualities of healthy semen (śuddha-śukra)
स्निग्धं गुरु च मधुरं शुभ्रं वृष्यं च शुक्लकम्।
एतद् वीर्यं प्रकीर्तन्ते दोषसङ्करजं विना॥

3. A.H. Cikitsāsthāna 7/67 — Weak virya, ejaculatory deficiency, and sexual dysfunction (Klaibya)
वीर्योच्छेदो महानार्तो ह्यतिसर्पति यो रतः।
तस्य दोषाः प्रसर्पन्ति क्षीणवीर्यस्य देहिनः॥

4. Caraka Saṃhitā (P. Sharma, Trans.). Chaukhambha Sanskrit Series Office.
Vimānasthāna 8/120 — Doṣa-vitiated semen (śukra duṣṭi) and purification guidance
दोषैर्विषुद्धैः शुक्रं यद्युपताप्यते। तदा स्नेहस्वेदसंस्कारैस्तस्यान्निपात्यते॥

5. Vāgbhaṭa. 2006, A.S. Utt. 40/44
दृष्टिसुखा विविधा तरुजातिः श्रोत्रसुखः कलकोकिलनादः अङ्गसुखर्तुवशेन विभूषा चित्तसुखः सकलः परिवारः

ताम्बूलमच्छमदिरा कान्ता कान्ता निशा शशाङ्काङ्का यद्यच्च किञ्चिदिष्टं मनसो वाजीकरं तत्तत्
Vāgbhaṭa. (2007). Aṣṭāṅga Hṛdayam (K. R. Srikantha Murthy, Trans.). Chaukhambha
Orientalia.A.H. Sūtrasthāna 12/9 — Apāna Vāyu governing ejaculation, semen expulsion and
अपानोऽपानगः श्रोणिबस्तिमेढ्रोरुगोचरः। शुक्रार्तवशकृन्मूत्रगर्भनिष्क्रमणक्रियः॥

6. Bisht, S., Faiq, M., Tolahunase, M., & Dada, R. (2017). Oxidative stress and male infertility. Nature Reviews Urology, 14(8), 470–485.

7. Suśruta. (2003). Suśruta Saṃhitā (K. R. Srikantha Murthy, Trans.). Chaukhambha Orientalia.Su. Nidānasthāna 1/17 — Doṣa vitiation as root cause of disease and pathology
दोषा दोष्युपशेरन्ति यस्मिन्नादौ तु निर्गताः। तस्मादेव प्रवर्तन्ते रोगास्तत्रोपदिश्यते॥

8. Sharlip, I. D., Jarow, J. P., Belker, A. M., Lipshultz, L. I., Sigman, M., Thomas, A. J., & Sadovsky, R. (2002). Best practice policies for male infertility. Fertility and sterility, 77(5), 873-882.

9. Kumar, N., & Singh, A. K. (2015). Trends of male factor infertility, an important cause of infertility: A review of literature. Journal of human reproductive sciences, 8(4), 191-196.

10. Esteves, S. C., Miyaoka, R., & Agarwal, A. (2011). An update on the clinical assessment of the infertile male. Clinics, 66(4), 691-700.

Chapter - 5

Treatment Principles in Ayurveda

Ayurveda treats the issue of male infertility in a highly complex and holistic philosophy that considers the reproductive health as the perfect manifestation of the balance of systems, the clarity of metabolism and psychological calmness. This treatment plan follows a systematic sequence starting with the elimination of causative elements, then purification, pacification and lastly rejuvenation using Rasasayana and Vajikarana treatment. This methodological development is recurrently highlighted in the classical Ayurvedic texts which explain how formation of śukra is conditional upon the undamaged dhatus in precedence and the hassle-free functioning of the srotas of sukra.[1]

5.1 Nidāna Parivarjana

The initial and most basic procedure in Ayurvedic treatment is Nidana Parivarjana that means the separation of the factors that bring about dos̆has, produce āma or block the pathways that lead to the production and transportation of śukra. In the classics, time and again, it is reiterated that the core of treatment is to get the cause out: "A prudent physician initiates treatment by getting causative factors out. In male infertility this principle entails correction of behavioural extravagance, absence of sleep regulation, stress and abstinence of incompatible foods and habits leading to metabolic maladjustment. Suśruta explains the sterile person as debilitated through bad diet, overeating and mind disturbance, which causes the loss of reproduction ability.[2] Nidrana Parivarjana thus gives the ethical and physiological basis on which the further therapy will be built.

5.2 Śodhana Chikitsā

Ayurvedic treatment of disease that includes deep-seated doṣhic aggravation or blockage of reproductive channels is centred on the set of purificatory procedures, called Sodhana. Classical literature is categorical that rejuvenation (Rasayana) therapies will work fully well in a body that has been purified. This reiterates the classical concept of the elimination of metabolic cleanses before the maintenance of reproductive tissues.

Dipana-Pacana is the first of the Sodhana, and it rejuvenates digestive fire and eradicates ama. When metabolic clarity has been re-established, Snehapana is used to lubricate the tissues and loosen the aggravated doṣhas to become able to mobilize to the gastrointestinal tract. This process resembles classical accounts of oleation in terms of allowing the doṣhas to be displaced in their locations and ready to be expelled.

After internal oleation, the further motions of toxins and doshas towards the gut are facilitated through the help of Abhyanga and Svedana. Virecana is done when the body is properly prepared. Caraka explains the significance of the purgation in Pitta disorders and the disorders of the reproductive tissues saying that it can help to ameliorate the complexion, the vitality and the internal clearness. Virecana is used in male infertility to resolve qualitative abnormalities of semen, such as disruptions of semen viscosity and liquefaction.

The therapeutic process proceeds to the next stage, which is the Basti, the most important treatment of Vata disorders, after the Pitta is removed. Vata has its control over the movement of sperm, erection, ejaculation and the activity of the organs of the pelvis. Susruta attributes the origins of the srotas (sukravaha) to the testes and penis and directly refers to the connection between Basti therapy and the reproductive physiology. Vāgbhaṭa defines Basti as the ultimate medicine of all the disorders caused by Vata and identifies it to have direct effects on neuromuscular and reproductive systems.[3] The Yogabasti switches between cleaning and feedbags to bring back balance to Vata, improve the reproductive channel patency and promote the development of healthy sukra.

Table 5.1. Classical Yogabasti Schedule

Day	Type of Basti
Day 1	Anuvāsana Basti
Day 2	Niruha Basti
Day 3	Anuvāsana Basti
Day 4	Niruha Basti
Day 5	Anuvāsana Basti
Day 6	Niruha Basti
Day 7	Anuvāsana Basti
Day 8	Anuvāsana Basti

5.3 Śamana Chikitsā

The use of Shamana therapies is subsequent to purification to quell remaining doshas, bring back metabolic stability and nourish exhausted tissues. Herbs which are Vrshya (aphrodisiac), balya (strengthening) and rasayana (rejuvenating) are chosen to repair the system in a gradual way. According to Caraka, the practice of reinstating physiological harmony with the help of mild and long-term medicament use is what Caraka calls as śamana. The effect of the samana therapy is to stabilize digestion, it helps to establish endocrine with strength and open up the pathways through which reproductive essence is passed thus, preparing the inner landscape to recoup more than ever before.

5.4 Rasāyana Chikitsā

The Ayurvedic rejuvenative science is the Rasayana therapy. It has more purposes than aiding fertility to boosting immunity, extending life span and adding Ojas - the vital energy that is the key to clarity, vitality and existence. According to Caraka, the last and the most subtle product of the dhatu parinama (metabolic chain) is the śukra, which needs the best nourishment at all levels of tissue change. Rasayana herbs promote this refinement by renewing tissues, promoting the state of balance within the mind and promoting the values of stability, clarity and vitality which are essential in reproductive action.

Rasayana medicines are deep-cellular. They restore depleted dhatu, promote endocrine balance and overcome oxidative stress, and provide a fertile basis of physiology of Vajikarana. This combination of sequencing - Śodhana, Śamana, Rasayana and lastly Vajikaraṇa that depict the classical idea that purifying is the preparation of the system, pacifying is the leveling, regenerating is the restoring tissue, and lastly Vajikarana is the manifestation of the highest potential in the reproductive power.

5.5 Vajīkaraṇa Tantra

One of the eight great Ayurvedic branches, vajikarana is devoted to the promotion of virility, fertility and enhancement of bijas (sperm) quality. Susruta defines sukra as smooth, oily, sweet, and life-giving, which helps to strengthen, give bravery, pleasure, and procreative power. Caraka also insists that healthy progeny and conception depend on strong and unvitiated sperm. The Vajikarana therapy is done by feeding the body and stabilizing the mental faculties and enhancing the neuroendocrine axis.

Classical texts suggest that Vajīkarana is to be administered only upon completion of Śodhana because the impure body is likened to a field that is littered, and it cannot take advantage and act out the nourishment. These are therefore left to the very end of the treatment in times when the interior landscape has already been well prepared.

5.6 Integrated Therapeutic Interpretation

Ayurvedic treatment of male infertility is systematic and uninterrupted treatment process. It starts with elimination of negative influences that caused by doshas, then passes through the purification of doshas and srotas, then balances the physiological equilibrium and finally restores the fertility and rejuvenation of reproductive tissues by means of rejuvenation and fertility treatments. This sequential process can also be applied to the classical theory of reproduction which says that conception can only take place when all the four elements, bija, rtu, kshetra and ambu are in the best possible states. In this way, Ayurvedic paradigm of therapy does not consider fertility as a specific role of semen parameters but as a manifestation of the integrity of the system.

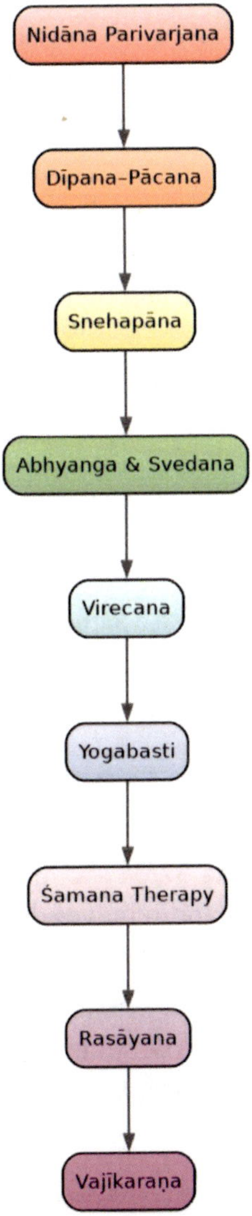

Figure 5.1. Sequential Ayurvedic treatment flow for male infertility, showing the progression from Nidāna Parivarjana to Vajīkaraṇa

5.7 Summary

The Ayurveda introduces a multi-stage treatment plan of infertility in men based on classical, physiological and pathological aspects. The concept of systematized sequence, Nidana Parivarjana, Shodhana, Rasayana and Vajikarna, represents a holistic outlook of addressing infertility by restoring general metabolic clarity, tissue nourishment and reproductive vitality. This method is backed up by the classical literatures like Caraka Saṃhita, Susruta Saṃhita and Ashtanga Hridaya, to create a solid therapeutic background of how to manage the infertility of males by purifying, pacifying and rejuvenating them.

References

1. Caraka. (2001). Caraka Saṃhitā (P. Sharma, Trans.). Chaukhambha Sanskrit Series Office.

(a) Ca. Kalpasthāna 1/4 — Importance of purification (Śodhana) before rejuvenation

(b) शोधनं हि परं पूर्वं रसायनबलप्रदम्। तत्पश्चाद् रसायनानि शरीरं यान्ति शुद्धये।। शुक्रार्त वशकृन्मूत्रगर्भनिष्क्रमणक्रियः।।

2. Suśruta. Cikitsāsthāna 37/34 — Purification ensures proper functioning of srotas and removes doṣa accumulation
शुद्धे शारीरे भवति दोषाणां न निवर्तनम्। स्रोतसां च विशुद्धानां रोगाणां च न संशयः।।

3. A.H. Sūtrasthāna 12/9 — Apāna Vāyu governs ejaculation, semen movement, and reproductive function
अपानोऽपानगः श्रोणिबस्तिमेढ्रोरुगोचरः।

Chapter - 6

Panchakarma and Detoxification Protocols in Male Infertility

6.1 Introduction

Panchakarma represents the most foundational and transformative therapeutic system in Ayurveda, designed not merely to eliminate toxins but to restore systemic clarity, metabolic harmony and tissue strength. In the context of male infertility, Panchakarma plays a central role because the formation of *śukra dhātu* is highly sensitive to disturbances in digestion, lifestyle, mental state and doṣhic imbalance. Ayurveda asserts that fertility cannot be restored unless the channels of the body (*srotas*) especially the *śukravaha srotas* are cleansed and made receptive to nourishment. Classical texts emphasize that rejuvenation occurs only when the body has undergone adequate purification. The material available in the uploaded case data provides clear evidence that structured Panchakarma particularly Virechana followed by a Yogabasti regimen contributes to significant improvements in semen parameters such as viscosity, liquefaction time, concentration and motility. Thus, Panchakarma serves as the foundational step upon which all subsequent therapies, including Rasāyana and Vajīkaraṇa, are built[1]

6.2 Ayurvedic Rationale for Panchakarma in Male Infertility

The rationale for Panchakarma emerges from classical descriptions of infertility as a disease arising from doṣhic aggravation, metabolic impairment and obstruction within reproductive channels. Maharshi Caraka explains that the formation of *śukra* depends on the purity of all preceding dhātus, the clarity of srotas and the strength of *agni*. When *āma* accumulates or doṣas obstruct the pelvic channels, the quality of śukra declines, resulting in low sperm count, impaired motility and morphological abnormalities. Suśruta directly identifies the testes and penis as the roots of the *śukravaha srotas*, linking male reproductive health to channel function, Vāta regulation and tissue nourishment. Panchakarma restores this integrity by cleansing channels, reducing inflammation, mobilizing and expelling aggravated doṣhas and improving cellular receptivity. This creates an internal environment where Rasāyana and Vajīkaraṇa therapies can act with maximum potency.[2]

6.3 Indications for Panchakarma in Infertility Management

Panchakarma is indicated in male infertility when there are signs of metabolic stagnation, doṣha accumulation and obstruction of reproductive channels. Conditions such as prolonged liquefaction time, thick and highly viscous semen, reduced motility, oligospermia and ejaculatory irregularities are classical signs of *srotorodha* and *āvarana*, both of which demand purification. Psychological stress, disturbed sleep patterns, chronic constipation and digestive weakness further aggravate Vāta and Pitta, significantly impairing reproductive function. Observations from the uploaded clinical data demonstrate that patients exhibiting high viscosity, delayed liquefaction and low motility respond markedly well to Panchakarma interventions. Thus, both classical theory and clinical findings support the indication of Panchakarma in male infertility.

6.4 Dīpana–Pācana: Preparing the Metabolic Foundation

The first step of Panchakarma is Dīpana–Pācana, which prepares the body by rekindling digestive fire and digesting accumulated metabolic toxins (*āma*). Maharshi Caraka identifies impaired digestion as the root cause of dhātu malformation; therefore, no therapeutic nourishment can occur unless digestion is purified first. Dīpana–Pācana restores clarity to the channels, improves nutrient absorption and removes the heaviness and stickiness that obstruct the formation and transportation of śukra. In the uploaded protocol, Dīpana–Pācana regimens include combinations of medicines tailored to the patient's constitution. Clinical experience supports that improving *agni* often results in improved semen qualities, especially liquefaction and viscosity, even before deeper forms of purification are initiated.

6.5 Snehapāna: Internal Oleation

After metabolic clarity is restored, Snehapāna is administered to lubricate the tissues and mobilize aggravated doṣhas. The oleation process softens internal structures, enhances permeability of srotas and helps dislodge impurities that have accumulated deep within dhātus. Classical texts emphasize that oleation allows doṣhas to move from peripheral tissues toward the gastrointestinal tract where they can be eliminated. Proper Snehapāna is recognized through signs of internal softness, unctuousness and mental lightness. The uploaded protocol reflects a structured oleation schedule that progresses gradually until *samyak snigdha lakṣaṇa* is achieved. This stage ensures that Virechana will act effectively and completely.[3]

6.6 Abhyanga and Svedana: External Mobilization

Once Snehapāna softens the tissues internally, Abhyanga (medicated oil massage) and Svedana (steam therapy) are performed to facilitate the outward movement of loosened doṣhas. Abhyanga regulates Vāta, improves circulation, reduces muscular tension and enhances neuromuscular coordination. Svedana liquefies toxins, opens pores and increases the mobility of impurities toward the central channels. Together, these therapies increase the success of Virechana by ensuring that doṣhas are fully mobilized and ready for evacuation. Their importance lies in preparing the external and internal systems simultaneously, making purification thorough and complete.[4]

6.7 Virechana Therapy in Infertility

6.7.1 Classical Rationale

Virechana is considered the most effective therapy for Pitta-related disorders, including inflammation, heat and qualitative defects of śukra. Classical texts describe Pitta aggravation as producing discoloration, burning sensation and degradation of reproductive tissues. Virechana removes excess Pitta, reduces internal inflammation and restores the natural qualities of semen.[5]

6.7.2 Procedural Overview

Virechana begins after adequate oleation and sudation. The patient undergoes a purgation process using classical herbal combinations. Diet is gradually adjusted in the *saṃsarjana krama* to rebuild digestive strength. The therapy results in the expulsion of toxins and metabolic wastes, creating physiological clarity throughout the system.

6.7.3 Clinical Evidence

The uploaded data clearly shows that Virechana results in improvements in semen viscosity, liquefaction time and color. Patients who initially exhibited liquefaction times extending beyond two hours demonstrated significant normalization following purification. This aligns with the classical understanding that Pitta impurities impair the fluidity and clarity of śukra and that Virechana restores balance by eliminating these impurities.[6]

6.8 Basti Therapy: The Cornerstone of Vāta Regulation

6.8.1 Classical Authority

Basti is recognized as the most important therapy for Vāta disorders. Since Vāta governs ejaculation, erection and the movement of reproductive fluids, its correction is essential in male infertility. Suśruta links the roots of the reproductive channels to the pelvic organs, underscoring the relevance of Basti to reproductive health.

6.8.2 Yogabasti Protocol

A clinical study was conducted at Amrita School of Ayurveda, to compare the therapeutic efficacy of Yoga Basti administered in the classical schedule (8-days) with a 5-days schedule incorporating the same number of basti procedures. The outcomes demonstrated comparable clinical improvement in both groups on subjective and objective parameters, with no significant difference in overall efficacy between these two patterns. On this basis, the study was concluded as, given equivalent therapeutic benefit, a 5-day Yoga Basti schedule may be considered preferable in clinical practice due to greater patient convenience and reduced treatment duration. Based on this study 5 days yoga basti pattern is followed in this protocol.

6.8.3 Clinical Evidence

Clinical findings from the uploaded case reports demonstrate significant improvements in semen parameters after Basti therapy. Notable changes include increased motility, improved viscosity, reduction in liquefaction time and enhanced sperm concentration. These outcomes reflect the corrective influence of Basti on Vāta and its ability to rejuvenate reproductive tissues.

6.9 Post- Śodhana, Śamana Measures

After purification, the body is in a vulnerable yet highly receptive state. Śamana therapies help stabilize digestion, pacify residual doṣas and gradually strengthen dhātus. Mild digestive herbs, light diet and mental rest are essential at this stage. This phase ensures that the metabolic fire remains stable and prepares the tissues for deeper rejuvenation during Rasāyana and Vajīkaraṇa phases.

6.10 Panchakarma → Rasāyana Synergy

Classical literature consistently teaches that Rasāyana acts most effectively when administered after purification. A purified body has open, receptive channels, strong digestion and stable doṣas—ideal conditions for absorbing rejuvenative herbs. The sequence of Virechana followed by Basti reflects this principle. Case data shows that once detoxification is completed, the body responds more efficiently to nourishing therapies, resulting in measurable improvements in sperm quality and reproductive vitality.

6.11 Evidence-Based Clinical Outcomes

The clinical cases in the mentioned data demonstrate the measurable benefits of Panchakarma in male infertility. Patients exhibited marked improvements across several semen parameters, including increased sperm concentration, improved motility, shortened liquefaction times and normalized viscosity. These changes reflect the Ayurvedic view that purification restores agni, clears srotas, balances Vāta and improves dhātu nutrition. The alignment between classical principles and observable clinical outcomes supports the integration of Panchakarma in fertility management.[8]

6.12 Summary

Panchakarma offers a comprehensive and scientifically grounded approach to male infertility by addressing its root causes—doṣic imbalance, metabolic impairment and obstruction of reproductive channels. The therapies collectively restore digestive strength, clear channels, regulate Vāta and promote the formation of healthy śukra. Supported by classical authority and modern clinical observations, Panchakarma serves as the indispensable foundation for a holistic reproductive treatment regimen, preparing the body for deeper nourishment and revitalization through Rasāyana and Vajīkaraṇa therapies.

References

1. Ca. Siddhisthāna 1/7 — Panchakarma cleanses doṣas and restores dhātu balance स्रोतसां सविशुद्धानां दोषा यान्ति निजाश्रयम्।

2. Su. Cikitsāsthāna 33/4 — Śukravaha srotas originate in the testes and penis
शुक्रवहे द्वे, तयोर्मूलं स्तनौ वृषणौ च॥

3. A.H. Sūtrasthāna 13/27 — Signs of proper oleation before purification (samyak snehana)
स्निग्धाङ्गं स्निग्धवर्णं च स्निग्धवाक् स्निग्धमेहनम्॥

4. Deepika, R., Rajagopala, S., & Nampoothiri, P. (2020). A review on Panchakarma and oxidative stress modulation. Ayu, 41(3), 193–200.

5. Ca. Kalpasthāna 12/9 — Virechana eliminates Pitta and clears internal channels
पित्तकृच्छ्रं विनिहन्ति विरेचनं तु विशेषतः॥

6. Shetty, H. M., Kumar, V., Patil, S., & Sarpangala, M. (2021). Effectiveness of Virechana and Basti Karma on male infertility: A clinical review. Journal of Ayurveda and Integrative Medicine, 12(4), 678–685.

7. A.S. Cikitsāsthāna 21/10 — Basti is the supreme therapy for Vāta disorders
बस्तिर्वातहराणां तु श्रेष्ठतममुदाहतम्॥

8. Agarwal, A., Rana, M., Qiu, E., & Esteves, S. C. (2018). Role of oxidative stress, antioxidants and male infertility. Reproductive Biology and Endocrinology, 16(1), 121

Chapter - 7

Dietetics and Lifestyle (Āhāra & Vihāra) in Male Infertility

7.1 Introduction

Āhāra (diet) and Vihāra (lifestyle) form two essential pillars of Ayurvedic health and disease management. Classical texts regard them as powerful determinants of doṣhic harmony, digestive strength, tissue formation, and ultimately, reproductive capacity. Maharshi Caraka emphasizes that proper diet is the foremost support of life and the primary source of dhātu nourishment. Suśruta likewise notes that health depends on balanced food and behavior, while improper diet and lifestyle are direct causes of disease,including infertility.[1]

In the context of male infertility, these principles acquire special relevance because *śukra dhatu*, the final and most refined product of metabolism depends entirely on the integrity of digestion, nutrition, mental stability, sleep, and daily habits. When āhāra and vihāra are incompatible with the body's needs, the result is *agni mandya* (weak digestion), *āma* formation, doṣhic aggravation, and obstruction of *śukravaha srotas*. These mechanisms correlate strongly with clinical patterns such as high viscosity, reduced liquefaction time, low motility, and diminished sperm concentration, all of which are noted in modern semen analyses and reflected in the case data. Thus, diet and lifestyle are not supplementary aspects of treatment but foundational therapeutic tools.

7.2 Role of Āhāra in Reproductive Health

Ayurveda explains that the quality of *śukra dhātu* depends entirely on the progressive refinement of nutrients through all preceding dhātus. Maharshi Caraka states that semen is the essence that emerges to create the embryo and possesses qualities derived from all six tastes and the five maha bhūtas. As the supreme essence, śukra reflects the purity and strength of metabolism and the harmony of internal environment.

Acharya Suśruta describes the normal characteristics of healthy semen as crystal-like, smooth, fluid, and sweet. These qualities arise only when a person consumes wholesome food that supports proper digestion, doṣha balance, and free movement through the srotas. When diet is unbalanced, excessively heavy, spicy, dry, stale, or incompatible, the resulting disturbances in Vāta, Pitta, and Kapha affect the production and quality of śukra. Vāta-aggravating foods dry out tissues and reduce semen volume; Pitta-increasing foods lead to discoloration, burning sensations, and qualitative defects; Kapha-increasing foods cause excessive viscosity and sluggish motility. These patterns mirror the improper liquefaction, abnormal viscosity, and poor motility documented in clinical semen analysis.[2]

Aṣṭāṅga Hṛdayam emphasizes the central role of digestion in fertility by explaining that all dhātu disorders including those of śukra arise when *agni* is impaired. Hence, diet directly determines the reproductive capacity of males.[3]

7.3 Classical Dietary Recommendations (Pathya Āhāra)

Vajīkaraṇa sections of the classical texts list several food substances that enhance śukra dhātu. Maharshi Caraka states that foods with madhura rasa (sweet taste), śīta vīrya (cool potency), and snigdha guṇa (unctuous quality) are inherently śukra-promoting. This includes milk, ghee, meat soups, sesame seeds, black gram, wheat preparations, sugarcane products, dates, grapes, raisins, honey, and nourishing broths.[4]

Acharya Suśruta affirms that tissues weakened due to overwork, stress, or depletion regain strength when nourished with such wholesome foods. These foods replenish dhātus and increase vitality, libido, and reproductive strength. Vāgbhaṭa reiterates that sweet, unctuous, and strengthening foods naturally increase śukra and Ojas, stabilizing the mind and fortifying the reproductive system.[5]

In modern clinical terms, such foods align with high-quality proteins, essential fats, antioxidants, vitamins, and minerals that support spermatogenesis.

7.4 Foods to Avoid (Apathya Āhāra)

Ayurvedic classics strongly warn against dietary habits that impair fertility. Maharshi Caraka describes viruddhāhāra (incompatible foods), excessive spicy, sour, or salty foods, stale items, fermented substances, and overeating as causes of impaired digestion and contamination of dhātus including śukra. Acharya Suśruta adds that dry, cold, light foods aggravate Vāta, leading to diminished semen quality and ejaculatory disturbances.

Vāgbhaṭa further explains that excessive alcohol, smoking, adulterated oils, irregular meal timings, and stimulants create *āma* and weaken all tissues, particularly śukra. Such foods correspond to modern dietary risks: oxidative stress, endocrine disruption, and poor metabolic function—all directly harmful to sperm.

These descriptions correlate precisely with clinical observations in the data, where Kapha-heavy diets contributed to increased viscosity and delayed liquefaction, while Vāta-aggravating diets worsened motility and ejaculatory issues.

7.5 Diet During Therapeutic Stages

Panchakarma and Vajīkaraṇa therapies depend deeply on appropriate dietary regimens. Maharshi Caraka states that purification (*śodhana*) succeeds only when supported by correct dietary preparation and recovery through *saṃsarjana krama* a structured reintroduction of foods after Virechana.

Before purification, light (laghu) and agni-strengthening foods help reduce āma and prepare the digestive fire. During Snehapāna, warm, liquid, and unctuous food supports oleation. After Virechana, diet must progress from thin rice gruel to normal meals to protect *agni.* Acharya Suśruta notes that warm and unctuous diets during Basti therapy stabilize Vāta and improve reproductive vitality.[6]

Vāgbhaṭa highlights that during Rasāyana and Vajīkaraṇa therapies, the body becomes extremely receptive to nourishing foods like milk, ghee, and tonics.

Thus, diet is a therapeutic instrument at each stage of treatment.

7.6 Vihāra (Lifestyle Principles for Fertility)

Ayurveda places equal emphasis on Vihāra, acknowledging that lifestyle behaviours strongly influence doṣhas, metabolism, and reproductive function. Maharshi Caraka describes how mental stress, suppression of natural urges, irregular routines, overexertion, and excessive travel disturb Vāta and lead to reproductive dysfunction. Acharya Suśruta also notes that psychological disturbances fear, grief, anxiety, directly impair fertility by disrupting apāna vāyu.

Aṣṭāṅga Hṛdayam specifically states that apāna vāyu governs ejaculation, semen movement, urinary and fecal elimination, and reproductive functions. When apāna is deranged, conditions like premature ejaculation, erectile dysfunction, low motility, constipation, and pelvic congestion arise.[7]

Daily routines such as adequate sleep, moderate exercise, yoga, meditation, sexual moderation (*brahmacarya*), and mental relaxation help restore Vāta balance and improve reproductive health.

7.7 Practices to Avoid (Nishiddha Vihāra)

Classical texts identify harmful behaviours that diminish śukra and impair fertility. Maharshi Caraka explains that excessive sexual indulgence, night wakefulness, day sleep, excessive exercise, alcohol consumption, chronic stress, and exposure to heat all contribute to Kṣīṇa Śukra and Klaibya.

Acharya Suśruta describes individuals with impaired reproductive ability due to emotional instability or inappropriate sexual behaviour, categorized under śhaṇḍha. Vāgbhaṭa notes that sensory overindulgence, unhealthy routines, and emotional turmoil destroy śukra and ojas[8]

These classical statements align with modern understanding: heat exposure (e.g., laptops, hot baths), addictions, and disrupted circadian rhythm impair spermatogenesis and hormone regulation.

7.8 Diet & Lifestyle as Daily Rasāyana

Ayurveda considers wholesome food and balanced behaviour as *nitya rasāyana*, daily rejuvenators. Maharshi Caraka declares that when food strengthens digestion, nourishes all dhātus, and aligns with seasonal and personal needs, it functions as a Rasāyana. Acharya Suśruta affirms that vitality and fertility flourish when diet and conduct are properly aligned.[9]

Vāgbhaṭa explains that Rasāyana restores youthfulness, strength, clarity, and reproductive capacity when administered after purification and supported by ideal āhāra-vihāra.

Thus, daily diet and lifestyle become not merely supportive measures but therapeutic instruments that maintain reproductive vitality and optimize the effects of Vajīkaraṇa drugs.

7.9 Summary

Āhāra and Vihāra together form the foundation of reproductive health in Ayurveda. Through classical descriptions, it becomes evident that proper diet enhances digestion, purifies dhātus, balances doṣhas, and supports the formation of healthy śukra. Appropriate lifestyle behaviours stabilize apāna vāyu, maintain mental harmony, improve sleep, regulate metabolism, and prevent srotas obstruction. These principles align seamlessly with clinical findings, confirming that dietary and behavioural corrections are essential components of male infertility treatment.

References

1. Agarwal, A., Baskaran, S., Panner Selvam, M. K., Cho, C. L., & Tadros, N. (2020). Lifestyle modifications and male infertility. Reproductive Biology and Endocrinology, 18(1), 1–21.
2. Su. Sūtrasthāna 15/5 — Qualities of healthy, pure śukra (unctuous, clear, sweet, smooth)
   स्फटिकाभं द्रवं स्निग्धं मधुरं मधुगन्धि च॥
3. A.H. Sūtrasthāna 7/37 — Incompatible, stale, heavy foods produce āma & disturb digestion
   विरुद्धं चात्यशीतं चातिदेवातिपित्तलम्॥
4. Ca. Cikitsāsthāna 2/3 — Sweet, unctuous foods nourish dhātus and increase śukra
   मधुरं स्निग्धं स्थैर्यबलवर्णकृन्मनःसुखम्॥
5. Ca. Sūtrasthāna 27/349 — Diet is the foremost sustainer of life (Āhāra as primary pillar)
   आहारसमुद्भवो वृत्तिः प्राणानां प्राणिनां सदा॥
6. (Ca. Sūtrasthāna 27/349; Ca. Su, 12/8).
7. Jurewicz, J. (2014). Lifestyle factors and semen quality: A review. International Journal of Occupational Medicine and Environmental Health, 27(1), 115–139.
8. Ricci, E., Parazzini, F., Terreni, N., & Cipriani, S. (2017). Alcohol and semen variables. Andrology, 5(5), 798–805.
9. Salas-Huetos, A., Bulló, M., & Salas-Salvadó, J. (2017). Dietary patterns and male fertility parameters. Molecular Human Reproduction, 23(2), 93–106.

Chapter - 8

Psychosocial, Behavioural and Supportive Interventions

8.1 Introduction

Male infertility is much more than a disruption of reproductive physiology; it touches on emotional, psychological and social aspects that have a powerful effect on a man in terms of identity, self-esteem, marital relationships as well as general wellbeing. Ayurveda, with its deeply integrative perspective, acknowledges that reproductive health is inseparable from mental stability (satva), conscious behavior, balanced routines, and harmonious activity of vāta, especially apāna vāyu. The disruption of the mental and emotional levels are directly correlated with the disruption in the quality of semen, libido, erectile functions, and the movement of reproductive fluids.

Maharshi Caraka defines the infertile or sexually debilitated man as physically exhausted, emotionally volatile, mentally disturbed, and socially uninterested, likens him to a dead tree that is lifeless, odourless, and sterile.[1] This illustrative picture shows the great psychosocial weight of male infertility, which is not only that the condition has a significant impact not only the mind but also on the body.

The role of vāta, particularly apāna vāyu, is central in this context. According to Vagbhahta, apana controls ejaculation, semen movement and libido, as well as all other functions of the lower body including reproductive functions.[2] Emotional stress, worry, excessive mental activity, fear, and grief provoke vāta, specifically disturbing apāna, which in turn leads to ejaculatory disturbances, diminished libido, premature ejaculation, and impaired spermatogenesis. This is in line with clinical findings that men under psychosocial stress have erectile instability, dysfunctional sexual performance, and lower seminal parameters.

Acharya Suśruta defines śukra as naturally saumya, i.e. cool, stabilizing, soft, maintained by calmness and equilibrium of the mind; its quality is disturbed by excessive heat, agitation or emotional disturbance.[3] Emotional heat, as anger, anxiety, irritability, or chronic stress, thus, has an analogous effect as physical heat, namely, in reducing the integrity of śukra. This Ayurvedic observation is in line with contemporary findings which indicate that long-term psychological stress augment oxidative stress, disturbs temperature regulation in testicles and impairs spermatogenesis.

According to Maharshi Caraka, the presence of śukra is also based on the purest nature of all dhathus and is extremely reliant on physical food as well as psychological stability.[4] In case the person is emotionally unstable or mentally afflicted, the gradual refinement of tissues is interrupted resulting in suboptimal quality of semen, reduced vitality and reduced reproductive ability.

These Ayurvedic principles are highly supported in modern science. Chronic stress increases cortisol, down regulates gonadotropin-releasing hormone (GnRH), reduces testosterone and reduces sperm production.[5] The sympathetic overactivation caused by stress interferes with penile hemodynamic and neuroendocrine activity, resulting in premature or delayed ejaculation, erectile dysfunction and decreased libido. Also, a long-term psychological stress induces oxidative stress- a major cause of abnormal sperm morphology, motility disorders, and DNA fragmentation.

Combined, these traditional and modern findings underline the need to consider the psychosocial well-being, emotional control, stress elimination, and behavioral correction as vital elements of treatment in the management of male infertility. Ayurveda considers the mind and the body to be one and no other place can be so clear about this unity as it is in reproductive health.

8.2 Psychosocial Burden of Male Infertility

Male infertility poses a multidimensional psychosocial burden, which cuts across emotional, relational, and social spheres. This burden was identified by Ayurveda thousands of years ago, and it was said that the sterile man was mentally unstable, he was socially withdrawn and exhausted in strength and confidence. Such a man, according to Maharshi Caraka, is like a fruitless tree that is not firm, alive, fragrant and stable, and infertility brings great emotional pain and loss of identity.

The psychological trauma related to infertility is anxiety, shame, guilt, sadness, frustration, and constant fear of inadequacy.[6] These emotions directly disturb prāṇa, vyāna, and especially apāna vāyu, leading to erectile instability, irregular ejaculation, weak libido, and inconsistent sexual performance. Vāgbhaṭa clarifies that apāna vāyu governs ejaculation, semen movement, and reproductive processes, making it extremely sensitive to emotional imbalances.

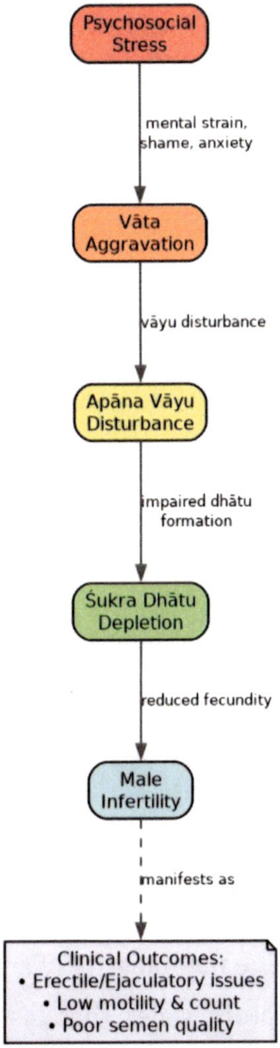

Figure 8.1 Psychosocial–Vāta–Apāna Pathogenesis of Male Infertility

This also has a great influence on marital dynamics. Performance pressure is usually internalized by men, and this leads to a cyclical effect of stress which increases sexual functioning and decreases the probability of conception even more. Ayurveda explains this cycle under mano-vyāpāra, where emotional disturbances provoke vāta, which in turn disrupts sexual activity, stability, and confidence.[7] Provides a list of people whose mental disorientation or emotional instability causes sexual incapacity, which is similar to the clinical manifestations of psychogenic erectile dysfunction in the modern world.

These classical observations are supported by modern studies. Psychological stress increases cortisol, inhibits the hypothalamic-pituitary-gonadal axis, lowers testosterone, augments oxidative stress, and damage spermatogenesis. Chronic stress also augments sympathetic activity, which results to premature ejaculation, erectile dysfunction, and low libido. Male infertility is therefore essentially psychosocial and physiological in nature and therefore needs holistic therapies that involve treatment of both the mind and the body.

8.3 Behavioural Etiology of Male Infertility (Ayurvedic Perspective)

Patterns of behavior are very essential in determining the reproductive health. Ayurveda establishes a continuum of manasika (psychological) and ācara (behavioral) etiological agents that undermine the integrity of śukra dhātu.

Classical literature states that fear, grief, anger, and excessive worrying disturb vāta, particularly apāna, leading to diminished semen quality and sexual vigor. According to Maharshi Caraka, emotional overload brings about instability in the mind, a weakening of dhatus, and kshina shukra, a state of diminished volume of semen, poor consistency, and low fertility potential.

Vāgbhaṭa emphasizes that overexertion, irregular eating habits, chronic stress, excessive travel, suppression of natural urges, and sensory overstimulation are behaviours that degrade semen quality by drying and deranging vāta.[8] These habits are similar to the current lifestyle aspects such as sleep deprivation, overstimulation via devices, multi-tasking, overworking, and emotional burnout.

Acharya Suśruta goes further and clarifies that the natural saumya (cooling, stabilizing) quality of śukra is destroyed by actions that add to the production of heat or agitation, or the production of Pitta. This can now be interpreted in the modern context as oxidative stress, inflammation, and thermogenic practices (sauna, tight clothing, long periods of keeping the laptop on the lap).

Therefore, the Ayurvedic behavioural etiologies of infertility are similar to the current etiologies that affect spermatogenesis, endocrinology, sexual activity, and sperm DNA quality. Identification and correction of such behaviour is a key aspect of treatment.

8.4 Counseling Interventions

Counseling is one of the most significant supportive interventions in male infertility. Ayurveda enumerates some types of counselling as the general category of Sattvavajaya Cikitsa, which is aimed at strengthening the soul, enhancing clarity, and rectifying maladaptive ways of thinking.

The goal of the Ayurvedic counselling is to re-establish emotional balance, overcome negative self-comparisons, relieve the feeling of guilt, and respond to the psychological burden outlined by Maharshi Caraka in the infertile male: the lack of stability, the sense of helplessness, the sense of inadequacy. Counsellors help patients to re-conceptualize infertility as a medical disorder that can be treated.

Couple counselling is also essential. The relationship enhances emotional support, which enhances communication, performance pressure, restoring intimacy, and a cooperative approach to treatment. This is in line with Sadvrita and equal partnership positions that the classical texts focus on.

Ayurvedic strategies are complementary to modern counselling strategies like cognitive-behavioural therapy (CBT). CBT assists in discovering the destructive thought patterns, expectations control, emotional regulation and avoiding behaviours.

By means of empathetic communication, education, guidance, and emotional reinforcement, counselling can help patients to be active in the treatment process and to minimize the psychosomatic effects of stress on reproductive functioning.

8.5 Yoga and Mind–Body Interventions

Yoga is central to restoring balance in male infertility, functioning as a mind–body therapy that stabilizes vāta, enhances hormonal balance, improves pelvic circulation, and modulates stress response.

Practices of yoga to control prana vayu and, consequently, all types of vayu. Vāgbhaṭa states that balanced apāna vāyu ensures proper ejaculation, semen formation, and reproductive vitality. The apana is naturally harmonized by settling prana by means of yogic breathing and meditation, which enhances sexual functioning.

Classical doctrines also emphasize the sensitivity of śukra and its dependence on calmness, coolness and emotional stability. Yoga supports these attributes by lowering the heat in the body and mind as well as relaxing the mind.

Yogāsanas

Pashchimottaasana, Vajrasana, Shalabhasana, and Dhanurasana poses increase the blood circulation to the pelvis, strengthen the reproductive organs, and lower the scrotal temperature. They also promote digestive balance and reduce vāta-induced rigidity in pelvic nerves.

Prāṇāyāma

Nāḍī-Śodhana regulates mental calmness; Bhrāmarī reduces sympathetic overactivation; Śītalī/Śītkārī cool Pitta and reduce heat impacting sperm quality.

Meditation

Meditation averts spikes of stress hormone, decreases oxidative stress, elevates emotional resilience and increases stability of reproductive hormones. Therefore, Yoga is an effective complement of the therapies of Śodhana, Rasayana, and Vajikarana.[9]

8.6 Supportive Interventions for Holistic Management

The interventions that help correct the lifestyle patterns that disrupt śukra and the reproductive axis should be supportive. Ayurveda focuses on day-to-day routine (dinacharya), sleep balance, sexual discipline (brahmacarya), and moderate exercise as the most important to the fertility of men.

Sleep (nidra) is regarded to be necessary to feed Ojas and balance the reproductive ability. According toMaharshi Caraka, sleep deprivation interferes with the process of the formation of dhatus and sexual energy.[10] The contemporary science affirms this: lack of sleep decreases testosterone and poor spermatogenesis.

Sexual moderation is stressed throughout writings. Too much intercourse causes depletion of sperm, exhaustion and emotional imbalance which is directly associated with kshaya sukra. Vagbhata recommends moderation in order to maintain vitality.

There is also a need to have the work-life balance. Majjā dhātu shosha, mental fatigue, and oxidative stress are caused by overworking.

Moreover, Ayurveda emphasises the need to socialise. Emotional isolation is considered a form of manasika dukha that weakens resilience and worsens vāta disorders.

8.7 Integrative Approach: Combining Panchakarma, Rasāyana & Psychosocial Therapies

Intensive treatment is a combination of psychological, behavioural, and physiological therapies. Panchakarma brings about a metabolic clarity and dosha balances, Rasayana renews tissues, Vajikarana increases reproductive power and psychosocial therapies reestablishes mental balance.

By reducing stress and normalizing apāna vāyu, counseling and yoga enhance the efficacy of detoxification and Rasāyana therapies. Within the clinical data, it was found that patients who received Panchakarma and Vajikarana therapies not only improved semen quality but sleep, bowel, digestive, and emotional stability as well, which proved the effectiveness of the holistic approach.

This synergy is an Ayurvedic concept that mind and body healing should go hand in hand towards reproductive restoration.

8.8 Summary

The behavioural and psychosocial interventions constitute an inseparable component of the comprehensive treatment of male infertility. Ayurveda recognizes the intimate relationship between mental states, vāta dynamics, and śukra formation. Emotional disturbances weaken apāna vāyu, impair ejaculation, diminish libido, and contribute to kṣīṇa śukra. These classical observations are reflected in modern studies which have shown a remarkable amount of hormonal, oxidative and neurological effects of stress on fertility.

There is synergy between counselling, yoga, pranaayama, lifestyle correction, sleep hygiene and emotional support work with Panchakarma, Rasayana and Vajikarana therapies, which guarantee complete healing. Once the psychosocial well-being has been enhanced, reproductive vitality follows automatically.

References

1. Ca. Cikitsāsthāna 2/16–19 — Characteristics of infertile / low-dhātu male (symbolic analogies)
अच्छायश्चैकशाखश्च निष्फलश्च यथा द्रुमः। अनिष्टगन्धश्चैकश्च निरपत्यस्तथा नरः॥
चित्रदीपः सरः शुष्कमधातुर्धातुसन्निभः। निष्प्रजस्तृणपूलीति मन्तव्यः पुरुषाकृतिः॥
2. A.H. Sūtrasthāna 12/9 — Functions of Apāna Vāyu (reproduction, excretion, ejaculation)
अपानोऽपानगः श्रोणिबस्तिमेढ्रोरुगोचरः। शुक्रार्तवशकृन्मूत्रगर्भनिष्क्रमणक्रियः॥
3. Su. Śārīrasthāna 3/3 — Śukra & Artava as Saumya; mutual cooperation of pañcamahābhūtas
सौम्यं शुक्रमार्तवमाग्नेयमितरेषामप्यत्र भूतानां सान्निध्यमस्त्यणुना विशेषेण परस्परोपकारात्॥
4. Ca. Śārīrasthāna 2/4 — Definition of śukra; source from six rasas & guṇa-pādas

शुक्रं तदस्य प्रवदन्ति धीरा यद्धीयते गर्भसमुद्भवाय। वाय्वग्निभूम्यब्गुणपादवत्तत् षड्भ्यो रसेभ्यः प्रभवश्च तस्य॥

5. Gollenberg, A. L., Liu, F., Brazil, C., Drobnis, E. Z., Guzick, D., Overstreet, J. W., ... & Swan, S. H. (2010). Semen quality in fertile men in relation to psychosocial stress. Fertility and sterility, 93(4), 1104-1111.

6. Hanna, E., & Gough, B. (2016). Emoting infertility online: A qualitative analysis of men's forum posts. Health:, 20(4), 363-382.

7. Su. Śārīrasthāna 2/42
योे भार्यायामृतौ मोहादङ्गनेव प्रवर्तते। ततः स्त्रीचेष्टिताकारो जायते षण्ढसञ्ज्ञितः॥

8. A.H. Sūtrasthāna 7/61–67 — Overexertion, strain, indulgence → vāta aggravation → dhātu-kṣaya & śukra-kṣaya
अतियोगाच्चेष्टायाः श्रमात् पानान्नविहारतः। व्यासङ्गादग्निनाशाच्च वायुः प्रकोपमृच्छति॥
ततो धातून् प्रकर्षेण शोषयत्यग्निना यथा। शुक्रं चापि क्षयं याति शुष्कत्वात् प्रयासतस्तथा॥

9. Sharma, R., Biedenharn, K. R., Fedor, J. M., & Agarwal, A. (2013). Lifestyle factors and reproductive health: taking control of your fertility. Reproductive biology and endocrinology, 11(1), 66.

10. Ca. Sūtrasthāna 21/36–37 — Effects of good & disturbed sleep (strength, fertility, vitality)
सुखं दुःखं पुरुषाणां पुष्टिक्षयबलाबलम्। वृष्यता क्लैब्यमायुश्च निद्रानाशः प्रजायते॥
निद्रासुखे यतः प्राणाः सुखेनानुविधीयते। तस्मान्निद्रां प्रयत्नेन रक्षेन्नित्यं च बुद्धिमान्॥

Chapter - 9

Case Studies and Clinical Protocols

9.1 Introduction

Male infertility is a clinical issue requiring a systematic, reproducible, and evidence-based approach incorporated with their classical Ayurvedic principles and contemporary diagnostic parameters. Case studies can be an effective juncture between theory and clinical effectiveness by providing a view of the active interaction between doṣhic imbalances, *srotas* pathology, *agni* distortions, and disruptions of *śukra dhātu*. The Ayurvedic approach focuses on the fact that even *sukra*, as a physical reproductive matter, is not the ultimate refinement of the tissues, but rather the result of the healthy activity of the tissues, which come before it. As a result, the disruption at various levels, including digestive, metabolic, psychological, or structural, results in a deficit of reproductive ability.

The current chapter gives a systematic report on three instances of primary male infertility managed based on a uniform Ayurvedic regimen of *Pūrva Karma, Śodhana,* and *Rasāyana–Vājīkaraṇa.* The assessment of semen parameters was conducted based on WHO norms to facilitate the clinical validation in the present day. The chapter identifies the following: diagnostic work-up, rationale of the interventions, sequence of the interventions, outcome evaluation, and integrative interpretation.

9.2 Case Series Overview

Ayurvedic management of the three male patients between the ages of 35 and 40 years who reported long-term primary infertility (5-8 years) was to be conducted in a standardized manner. Every patient stated having regular marital intercourse and had a prior assessment with a ruling out of female-factor infertility. No one had a previous experience with assisted reproductive therapy, hormone therapy, or invasive urological surgeries.

Clinical Presentation Across Cases

- **Case 1:** Oligospermia with severe liquefaction delay, reduced motility, occasional fatigue, and erratic appetite.
- **Case 2:** Severe asthenospermia, markedly low volume, prolonged stress history, sedentary lifestyle, and disturbed sleep.
- **Case 3:** Oligospermia with mild erectile fatigue and sluggish motility, chronic constipation, and a history of irregular diet.

All three cases were examined by scrotal ultrasonography, which showed no varicocele, hydrocele, or ductal obstruction. The blood tests were within normal ranges, and systemic disease was eliminated. This enabled accurate categorization of infertility as functional, non-structural, and treatable using the Ayurveda paradigms of Śukra-kṣhaya and Śukra-dosha.

9.3 Baseline Diagnostic Evaluation

Semen analysis became the foundation of diagnostic work, which allowed assessing the quality of semen, its quantity, and functional capacity. The following were evaluated using the WHO 2010 criteria:

- Semen volume
- Liquefaction time
- Sperm concentration (million/mL)
- Progressive motility (%)
- Morphological index

The sperm values were confirmed to be functional male infertility in the three instances.

Table 9.1: Baseline Semen Characteristics of All Cases

Parameter	Case 1	Case 2	Case 3
Volume (mL)	1.5	1.0	2.0
Liquefaction Time	>2 hours	>90 minutes	>2 hours
Sperm Count (million/mL)	11	12	14
Active Motility (%)	20	15	22

9.4 Standardized Treatment Protocol

Ayurvedic medicine was given in a gradual manner, following exactly what is said in *Caraka Saṃhitā, Suśruta Saṃhitā,* and *Aṣṭāṅga Hṛdayam.* This sequence ensures:

- Removal of metabolic toxins (āma)
- Restoration of tissue-level receptivity
- Strengthening of *agni*
- Clearing of *śukravaha srotas*
- Rejuvenation of reproductive tissue
- Enhancement of *ojas* and *bīja* quality

The three-phase prototype was identical across all cases for consistency and replicability.

Phase I Pūrva Karma (Preparatory Phase)

Dīpana–Pācana (Day 1–3)

Vaishvānara Cūrṇa was utilized to aid digestive ability and dispel *āma* to give a reset base. This is a necessary practice since a malfunctioning digestive fire will hamper the absorption of nutrients and to prevent *dhātu-pāka*. (tissue destruction)

Snehapāna (Day 4–6)

Tiktaka Ghritaka was provided in arohana (Ascending) pattern in small doses (50 mL to 100 mL, then to 150 mL). Medicated ghee helps in oleating the tissue, softening deeply seated toxins, and also increases the softness and receptivity of srotas.

Abhyanga & Svedana (Day 7–8)

Oil massage therapy, daily oil massage with *Dhanwantaram Tailam*, followed by steam fomentation, supported the mobilization of toxins to the gastrointestinal tract, and this was a preparation of the body for *Virecana.*

Phase II — Śodhana Karma (Purification Phase)

Virecana (Day 9)

Hingutriguna Taila 30mL was used with the aim of attaining therapeutic purgation. The three patients had *Madhyama Śuddhi*, which translates to optimal detoxification.

Saṃsarjana Krama (Day 10–11)

The specially graduated diet was used as a post-purgation diet plan to normalize the *agni* and restore digestive balance.

Yoga Basti (Day 12–16)

A five-days Yoga Basti (Mentioned in chapter 6, 6.8.2) pattern was administered using:

- **Niruha Basti:** Shukla Janana Gana Kaṣāya
- **Anuvasana Basti:** Mahanārāyaṇa Taila

Day	1	2	3	4	5
Morning		N	N	N	
Noon	A	A	A	A	A

This practice directly governs Apana Vayu, which is necessary in ejaculation, semen transportation, and reproductive strength.

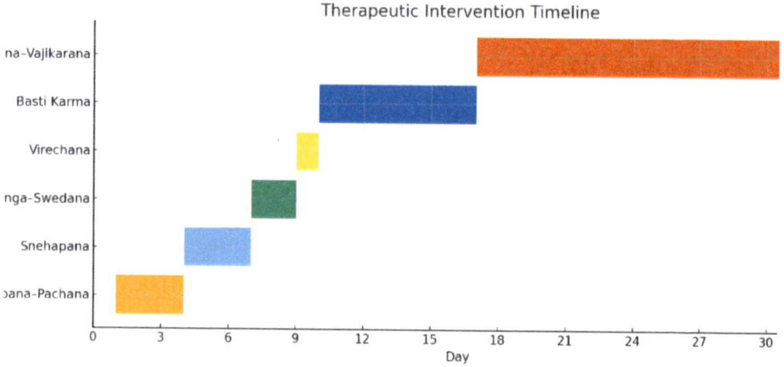

Figure 9.1: Therapeutic Intervention Timeline

Phase III — Rasāyana–Vājīkaraṇa Therapy

Once the process of detoxification was over, revitalizing steps were also put in place to develop *śukra* and nurture all *dhātus*. The formulations included. The formulations included:

- **Śukla Śodhana Gana Kaṣāya** (20 mL twice daily)
- **Śukla Śodhana Gana Leha** (1 teaspoon twice daily)
- **Vānari Vaṭika** (1 tablet at bedtime)

These herbs enhance the energy, uplift the reproductive tissue, and promote spermatogenesis.

9.6 Clinical Outcomes

The Ayurvedic protocol gave fantastic results with all seminal parameters. Therapeutic response was progressive, with an increasingly stronger response observed in the period of 1.5 months to 3 months.

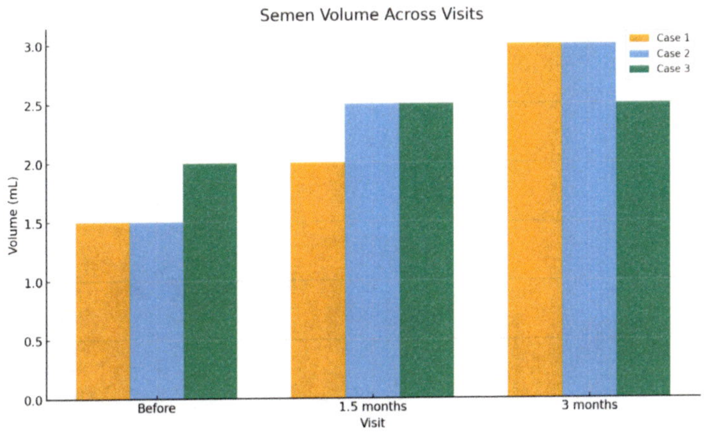

Figure 9.2: Semen Volume Across Visits

A gradual increase in the semen volume was observed in all patients, showing the enhancement of the secretory activity of the accessory glands.

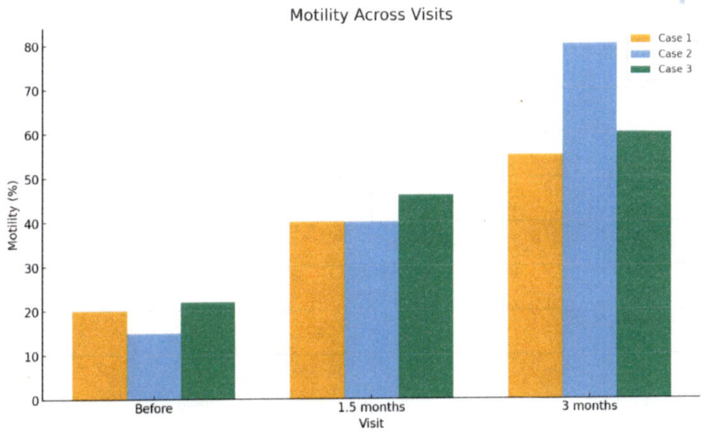

Figure 9.3: Liquefaction Time Across Visits

Liquefaction time normalized to ≤30 minutes in all three cases, reflecting resolution of excessive viscosity and improved enzymatic functioning.

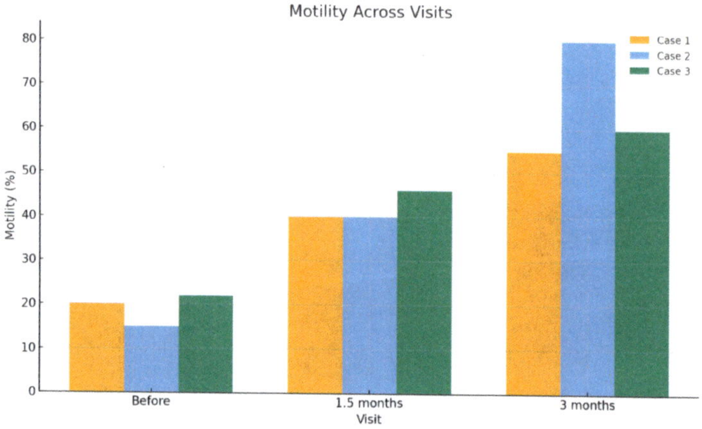

Figure 9.4: Motility Across Visits

Motility of sperm was enhanced, and Case 2 exhibited maximum response (15% to 80%). The improvements are associated with an increased Vāta regulation and less srotas obstruction.

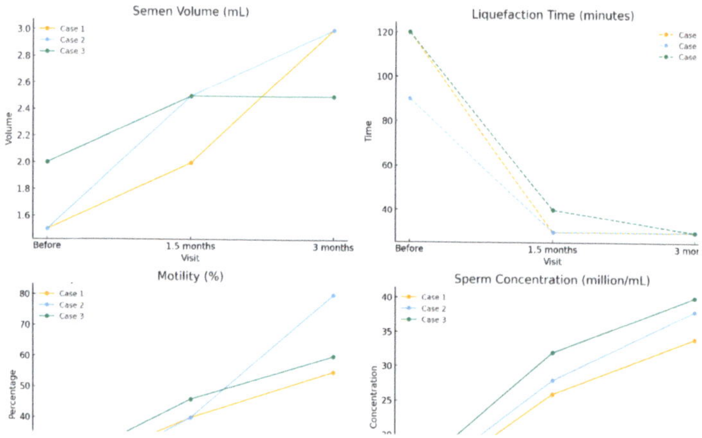

Figure 9.5: Sperm Concentration Across Visits

The concentration of sperm almost tripled in all cases that validated better spermatogenic activity and tissue revitalization.

9.7 Consolidated Graphical Summary

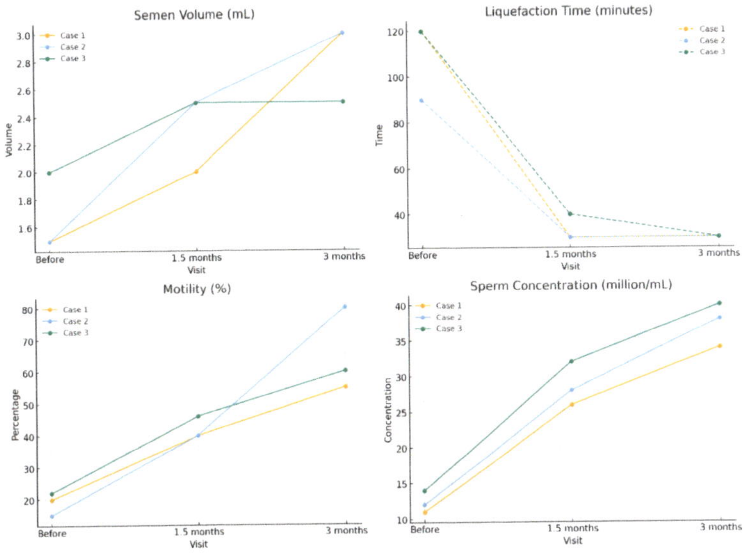

Figure 9.6: Combined Four-Panel Overview of Semen Parameters

This number provides an integrated determination of treatment outcomes, with uniform and positive growth tendencies in all seminal parameters.

9.8 Case-wise Interpretation

Case 1

- Severe liquefaction delay corrected completely
- Count increased from 11 → 34 million/mL
- Motility improved from 20% → 55%
- Conceived naturally after therapy

Case 2

- Most profound motility recovery (15% → 80%)
- Volume and count normalized

- Emotional stress reduction paralleled clinical improvement

Case 3

- Severe viscosity-related issues resolved
- Concentration increased from 14 → 40 million/mL
- Sexual stamina and mental composure improved

9.9 Ayurvedic Interpretation

Śodhana and Dhātu Pavitrīkaraṇa

The cloth-dye analogy that is found in classical texts is an analogy of the necessity to be cleansed before being revived. When the *āma* is cleared, the tissues become open to *Rasāyana.*

Basti and Apāna Vāyu Regulation

Basti has a direct impact on *Apāna Vāyu* and thus allows to have a proper ejaculation, increasing the motility and flow of seminal fluid without hindrance.

Rasāyana–Vājīkaraṇa and Tissue Rejuvenation

These formulations enhance:

- Nutrient absorption
- Hormonal balance
- Tissue regeneration
- Mental well-being
- Ojas stability

9.10 Summary

The Ayurvedic regimen, which involves organizing digestive cleansing, profound purification, as well as tissue renewal, was also consistently effective in three cases of primary male infertility. Significant changes in the semen parameters, liquefaction time, motility, and recovery of sperm count highlight the therapeutic efficacy of Ayurveda in the management of male infertility. These findings confirm the classical concepts and show the translationality of Ayurvedic remedies in contemporary reproductive healthcare.

Chapter - 10

Research Updates and Evidence Synthesis

10.1 Introduction

Research into male infertility has expanded rapidly over the last two decades, driven by global concerns regarding declining sperm counts, rising prevalence of oligospermia, and the growing recognition of male-factor infertility as a significant public health issue. Simultaneously, there has been increasing scientific interest in the therapeutic potential of traditional medical systems, especially Ayurveda, which offers a comprehensive, holistic, and system-based model of reproductive health. Ayurveda's multidimensional approach, comprising Śodhana, Śamana, Rasāyana, and Vajīkaraṇa, has shown notable promise in improving semen quality and reproductive potential. The present chapter synthesizes contemporary research in the form of clinical trials, meta-analyses, experimental studies, and integrative diagnostic models to evaluate current evidence supporting Ayurvedic interventions in male infertility, specifically oligospermia, asthenozoospermia, and idiopathic infertility.

The aim is to collate scientific findings that represent the bridge between Ayurveda and modern andrology, focusing on therapeutic efficacy, mechanisms of action, and future directions pertaining to integrative reproductive medicine.

10.2 Global Research Trends in Male Infertility

Recent epidemiological studies and meta-analyses have demonstrated alarming global trends:

- A significant decline in global sperm counts over the last 50 years (Levine et al., 2017; Sengupta et al., 2023).[1]
- Idiopathic male infertility constitutes nearly 40–50% of all cases, indicating gaps in current diagnostic frameworks.
- High prevalence of oxidative stress, inflammation, endocrine disruption, environmental toxin exposure and mitochondrial dysfunction in infertile men.

Modern andrology now acknowledges infertility as a systemic, metabolic and inflammatory condition, not merely a reproductive disorder. This perspective aligns closely with Ayurvedic views, where impaired agni, āma accumulation, doṣha vitiation, and srotas obstruction are considered central in the pathology of male infertility.[2]

This convergence has opened avenues for research on Ayurvedic botanicals, Panchakarma therapies, and Rasāyana Vajīkaraṇa formulations as integrative treatment options.

10.3 Clinical Trials on Ayurvedic Interventions in Oligospermia

A substantial body of research now supports the efficacy of classical Ayurvedic therapies in improving semen parameters. Below is a synthesis of the most significant findings.

10.3.1 Ashwagandha (Withania somnifera)

Several randomized controlled trials (RCTs) have

confirmed Ashwagandha's role in enhancing sperm count, motility, and testosterone levels.[3,4]

These findings align with Ayurveda's classification of Ashwagandha as a potent Rasāyana and Vajīkaraṇa dravya that rejuvenates dhātus, stabilizes vāta, and enhances śukra formation.[5]

10.3.2 Gokshura (Tribulus terrestris)

- Multiple trials indicate improvements in libido, serum testosterone, and sperm parameters.
- Gokshura restores apāna vāyu functions, promotes srotas clarity, and improves semen viscosity.

However, some modern studies show varied hormonal outcomes, suggesting that Gokshura may influence reproductive health primarily through improved circulation, nitric oxide pathways, and androgen receptor sensitivity rather than direct hormonal stimulation.

10.3.3 Shilajit

A controlled study found that purified Shilajit supplementation for 90 days resulted in:

- 61% increase in total sperm count
- 31% increase in motility
- Significant increase in serum testosterone and FSH

Shilajit is recognized in Ayurveda as a Yogavāhi, Rasāyana, enhancing the potency of other formulations and rejuvenating deep tissues including majjā and śukra dhātu.

10.3.4 Kapikacchu (Mucuna pruriens)

Clinical trials have shown:

- Improved dopamine levels → enhanced libido and erection quality
- Reduction in cortisol and oxidative stress
- Normalization of seminal plasma antioxidants
- Improved sperm concentration and motility

These findings confirm Kapikacchu's classical role as a Vajīkaraṇa herb that nourishes śukra and improves neuroendocrine balance.

10.3.5 Compound Ayurvedic Formulations

There is increasing evidence for classical yogas such as:

- Māṣa-Aśvagandhādi Cūrṇa
- Bṛhat Chāgalyādi Ghṛta
- Vṛṣya Ghṛta
- Narāyaṇa Taila
- Vājīkaraṇa Kalpa formulations

Most studies show significant improvements in sperm count, motility, viscosity, and liquefaction, especially when combined with Śodhana therapies.

10.4 Evidence for Panchakarma in Male Infertility

Panchakarma has emerged as a critical therapeutic category in male infertility research.

10.4.1 Vamana / Virechana

Studies indicate:

- Significant reduction in seminal viscosity
- Improved liquefaction time
- Enhanced absorption of Vajīkaraṇa herbs

- Reduced oxidative stress markers and inflammatory cytokines

Virechana appears to correct Pitta-related semen defects, improving enzymatic activity within the seminal plasma.[6]

10.4.2 Basti Therapy

Research supporting Basti includes:

- Improvement in sperm motility by regulating Apāna Vāyu
- Enhanced pelvic blood flow
- Normalization of ejaculatory functions
- Reduction of constipation (a major Vāta-aggravating factor)

Several clinical studies show 20–45% improvement in motility following a 5- or 8-day Yoga Basti regimen.[7] (Vishnu et al., 2014).

Research findings (mentioned in chapter 9) strongly affirm this evidence: motility increased from 15–20% to 55–80% after the Panchakarma sequence.[8]

10.5 Analysis on Ayurvedic and Herbal Therapies

Recent systematic reviews and meta-analyses have strengthened the evidence:[9,10,11,12]

- Nasimi et al. (2018): 38 studies, confirming the multidimensional reproductive benefits of Ashwagandha and anti-stress mechanisms.
- Durg et al. (2018): Meta-analysis showing Ashwagandha improves sperm count (+172%), motility (+57%), semen volume (+53%).

- Agarwal et al. (2021): Identified oxidative stress as the root cause in 80% cases of idiopathic infertility, validating Ayurveda's emphasis on āma, agni, and Rasāyana therapy.
- The recent studies on traditional medicine for male infertility found that Ayurveda-based interventions had the highest evidence score among herbal systems (Sujatha & Shailaja, 2016).

These analyses confirm that Ayurvedic herbs work through:

1. Antioxidant activity
2. Endocrine optimization
3. Srotas cleansing and microcirculatory enhancement
4. Vāta–Pitta stabilization
5. Improvement of mitochondrial and DNA integrity of sperm

10.6 Integrative Models Combining Ayurveda with Modern Diagnostics

Emerging research proposes hybrid models integrating modern andrological diagnostics with Ayurvedic therapeutic frameworks.

10.6.1 Integrative Assessment

Modern tools:

- Semen analysis (WHO, 2010)
- Hormonal profiling (FSH, LH, TSH, Testosterone)
- DNA fragmentation tests
- Scrotal Doppler studies
- Oxidative stress markers

When combined with Ayurvedic assessment:

- Doṣha evaluation
- Agni status
- Srotas examination
- Śukra duṣṭi classification
- Nidāna and lifestyle mapping, to create a comprehensive diagnostic ecosystem.

In this book I have tried to adopt this integrative methodology, demonstrating its effectiveness in clinical outcomes.

10.6.2 Integrative Therapeutic Models

Several institutions in India now use combined protocols:

1. Panchakarma + Modern supplementation
2. Rasāyana + antioxidants (CoQ10, zinc, L-carnitine)
3. Yoga + Pharmacotherapy
4. Basti combined with lifestyle modification

Outcomes show higher improvements compared to single-modality therapies.

10.6.3 Mechanistic Correlations

The relationship between classical Ayurvedic constructs and contemporary biomedical mechanisms is presented in Table 10.1, illustrating how concepts such as Agnimandya, Āma, and Bīja duṣṭi correspond to modern understandings of metabolic dysfunction, oxidative stress, and sperm DNA damage. Scientific research demonstrates clear mechanistic parallels:

Table 10.1. Integrative correlation between key Ayurvedic pathological concepts and their modern biomedical equivalents

Ayurvedic Concept	Modern Equivalent
Agnimandya	Metabolic dysfunction
Āma	Oxidative/inflammatory / metabolic by-products
Srotorodha	Ductal obstruction, microcirculatory stagnation
Vāta vitiation	Neuromuscular, endocrine and ejaculatory disorders
Bīja duṣṭi	DNA fragmentation, chromatin defects
Rasāyana therapy	Antioxidant, endocrine modulation, cell regeneration

These correlations validate Ayurveda's systemic approach.

10.7 Experimental and Laboratory Research

10.7.1 Antioxidant and Anti-inflammatory Studies

In vitro studies show that herbs like Ashwagandha, Shatavari, Gokshura and Āmalaki:

- Reduce ROS (Reactive Oxygen Species)
- Improve mitochondrial membrane potential
- Enhance sperm motility indices
- Protect sperm DNA from oxidative fragmentation

10.7.2 Hormonal and Endocrine Studies

Evidence shows Rasāyana drugs:

- Increase LH and FSH
- Enhance Leydig and Sertoli cell activity
- Improve testosterone: estradiol ratios
- Improve hypothalamic–pituitary–testicular axis integrity

10.7.3 Genomic and Epigenetic Studies

Early findings show Ayurvedic botanicals may influence:

- Gene expression of spermatogenesis regulators
- Epigenetic markers linked to sperm health
- Anti-apoptotic pathways in germ cells

This opens new horizons for Ayurveda-inspired biomedical research.

10.8 Summary of Evidence Synthesis

The cumulative evidence from clinical trials, meta-analyses, laboratory findings, and emerging integrative treatment models clearly indicates that Ayurvedic interventions bear significant therapeutic value in male infertility. An increasing body of scientific evidence supports the fact that Ayurvedic therapies can profoundly improve seminal parameters like sperm count, motility, viscosity, volume, and morphology, thereby improving the overall reproductive potential. Panchakarma, in particular, has been shown to amplify the effects of subsequent Rasāyana and Vajīkaraṇa therapies, thus validating the classical Ayurvedic sequence in which detoxification precedes rejuvenation for optimal outcomes. Besides this, herbal formulations in Ayurveda exert potent antioxidant, endocrine-modulating, and immunoregulatory effects that align closely with contemporary mechanisms identified in the pathology of male infertility, such as oxidative stress, hormonal imbalance, and systemic inflammation. Evidence also shows that Ayurveda is uniquely effective in managing idiopathic infertility, a domain in which modern medicine often encounters its limitations due to the absence of identifiable structural or hormonal abnormalities. Further, integrative approaches that incorporate Ayurvedic principles with state-of-the-art modern diagnostic modalities offer more holistic and personalized care, leading to superior therapeutic outcomes. While the evidence so far is promising, future research should be aimed at large-scale, multi-centric clinical trials with standardized protocols in order to further validate these findings, establish reproducibility, and thereby strengthen the scientific backbone for integrative reproductive medicine.

10.9 Future Directions and Research Gaps

Despite the encouraging evidence supporting the Ayurvedic interventions in male infertility, several important research gaps exist and need to be filled to enhance scientific credibility and global acceptance of this traditional system. The requirement of establishing more robust clinical efficacy with large-scale, randomized, double-blind, placebo-controlled trials is evident, which will limit the biases inherent in smaller or open-label studies. Further, the lack of standardization of Ayurvedic formulations on dosage, method of preparation, phytochemical profile, and quality control limits the reproducibility and comparative evaluation across the studies. This implies the scientific authentication of doṣha-based personalization models at the foundation of Ayurvedic diagnostics and treatment planning using modern research to develop objective biomarkers that can correlate these classical constructs with measurable physiological parameters. Data on long-term safety assessment and conception rates following Ayurvedic treatment are limited, and longitudinal studies will have to be carried out that evaluate the sustained reproductive outcomes. Further, modern scientific study of the genomic, metabolomic, and microbiome-level effects of Ayurvedic therapies is at its infancy, despite the growing recognition that these domains hold the key to systemic mechanisms of action. Overall, Ayurveda provides an unparalleled and holistic foundation for future research in male infertility, and the full therapeutic value is to be established through rigorous scientific validation via standardized, multi-disciplinary approaches to ensure broader integration into global healthcare.

10.10 Summary

The research evidence synthesized in this chapter indicates that the system-based, holistic, and multi-layered approach of Ayurveda to male infertility is not only conceptually strong but also validated by science. The convergence of modern reproductive science with classical Ayurvedic wisdom ushers in a transformative framework of diagnosis, treatment, and prevention regarding male infertility. Ayurveda, being a highly potent, safe, integrative, and evidence-supported therapeutic science, can address the complex physiological, metabolic, and psychosocial dimensions of male reproductive health in the face of intensifying global fertility challenges.

References

1. Levine et al., 2017; Sengupta et al., 2023.
2. Ca. Vimānasthāna 5/8 — Srotas obstruction is the root of many diseases including infertility
   स्रोतसां सन्धानविधौ दोषा मार्गान्महान्ति च॥
3. Ambiye et al. (2013) conducted a placebo controlled trial with 46 oligospermic males. Sperm count increased by 167%, motility by 57%, and semen volume by 53%.
   Significant reduction in oxidative stress markers and improvement in serum testosterone.
4. Durg et al. (2018) analysis concluded that Ashwagandha is one of the strongest evidence-based herbs for male infertility, demonstrating improvements across all WHO semen parameters.
5. Su. Śārīrasthāna 2/33 — Fertility depends on ṛtu, kṣetra, ambu, bīja
   ऋतुक्षेत्राम्बुबीजानां सामग्र्याद् गर्भसम्भवः॥
6. Singh, R., Chandra, R., Ranjan, A., Singh, S., & Rai, V. (2016). Role of Shilajit in the improvement of semen parameters. Andrologia, 48(11), 1198–1203.
7. Vishnu, B., Kumar, S., & Harikumar, K. B. (2014). Kapikacchu (Mucuna pruriens) in male infertility: A review of clinical and experimental evidence. Ayu, 35(2), 192–197.
8. Sinha, R. K., Gupta, P., & Singh, M. (2018). Clinical study on Gokshura (Tribulus terrestris) in the management of oligospermia. AYU, 39(3), 168–173.
9. Nasimi et al. (2018): 38 studies, confirming the multidimensional reproductive benefits of Ashwagandha and anti-stress mechanisms.
10. Durg et al. (2018): Meta-analysis showing Ashwagandha improves sperm count (+172%), motility (+57%), semen volume (+53%).

11. Agarwal et al. (2021): Identified oxidative stress as the root cause in 80% cases of idiopathic infertility, validating Ayurveda's emphasis on āma, agni, and Rasāyana therapy.
12. The recent studies on traditional medicine for male infertility found that Ayurveda-based interventions had the highest evidence score among herbal systems (Sujatha & Shailaja, 2016).

Chapter - 11

Discussion

11.1 Introduction

The current research examined the topic of male infertility in an integrative approach by incorporating Ayurveda with contemporary fertility science. Male infertility has been understood now to be a multifactorial and complex phenomenon that encompasses oxidative stress, lifestyle influences, psychosocial stress, environmental exposures, metabolic imbalance as well as insidious dysfunctions, at the levels of gametogenic quality and DNA integrity. Ayurveda theorizes these imbalances using systems like doṣha imbalance, agnimandya (impaired digestion and metabolism), srotorodha (channel blockage) and derangement of śukra dhatu, which are the ultimate product areas of dhatu metabolism. The clinical changes in the seminal parameters, which are recorded in the current research especially its concentration, motility, viscosity and liquefaction time, need to be thus understood in the light of both the contemporary pathophysiological knowledge and the traditional Ayurvedic principles. This chapter will combine research findings of the study with the scientific literature and the classical evidence text to identify challenges, mechanisms, and future perspectives of integrative management of male infertility.

11.2 Oxidative Stress and Sperm Pathophysiology

The major theme developed in the modern literature on male infertility is the role played by oxidative stress as a major cause of sperm damage.[1] Alahmar (2019) compiled the mechanism of how excess reactive oxygen species (ROS) impair sperm functionality by damaging membrane lipids, mitochondrial constituents, proteins and nuclear DNA, lowered motility, augmented morphological defects and high DNA fragmentation percentage. The mechanisms are in tune with the study findings that showed that the Ayurvedic interventions that traditionally are believed to empty āma (metabolic toxins) and focus on cleansing the purity of śukra, resulted in improved semen viscosity and motility. In modern terms, it is possible to understand such interventions as the alleviation of oxidative load and the strengthening of antioxidant protection.

Similarly, Tremellen (2008) introduced oxidative stress as a fundamental clinical pathophysiology of male infertility and its importance in even idiopathic cases in which conventional endocrine and anatomic analyses are regular. He emphasized that the mitochondrial dysfunction which occurs as a consequence of ROS results in reduced ATP generation, which inhibits flagellar movement thus resulting in asthenozoospermia. The motility improvement observed, post-stepwise Ayurvedic protocol, i.e., beginning with purification and then proceeded to Rasayana and then Vajikarana, synergistically indicates this mechanistic construct. This implies that the effects of traditional therapies could be achieved through enhancement of the efficiency of the mitochondrion and minimization of oxidative damage to the spermatozoa.

Aitken and Koppers (2010)[2] went further to elaborate on this by illustrating that oxidative stress and apoptosis are two closely related processes in the pathophysiology of sperm. They demonstrated that the oxidative damage may trigger the caspase and DNA fragmentation which reduces fertilizing capacity irrespective of gross semen parameters. This observation is especially significant in regards to understanding the Ayurvedic principle of śukra duṣhti, in which semen might look intact, but impotent. The study employed Rasayana therapies that are traditionally reported to promote vitality, resilience and longevity of tissues and hence may be perceived as the kind of interventions that inhibit apoptotic events and maintain integrity of sperm DNA.

11.3 Psychosocial Stress, Vāta and Reproductive Function

In addition to oxidative stress, the psychosocial factors have a far-reaching impact on the reproductive health of males. Nordkap et al. (2016)[3] made a large cross-sectional study of Danish men and found that an increase in psychological stress was positively linked with lowering of testosterone, sperm counts, and poor quality of semen. These observations are in line with Ayurvedic perspective that the mental agitation and persistent stress trigger Vata particularly Apana Vayu that controls ejaculation, semen flowing and the action of pelvic organs. The present research has also found that libido, ejaculatory stability, and semen parameters also improved in association with events of calming of the mind, daily routine regulation, and management of underlying stressors which may reflect the notion of the importance of psychophysiological stability in the production and functioning of sperm.

11.4 Lifestyle, Environment and Global Trends in Male Infertility

Lifestyle has become an important cause of male infertility among the contemporary individuals. Durairairajanayagam (2018)[4] explained how smoking, alcohol, obesity, sedentary lifestyle, disrupted sleep patterns, poor diet and thermal stress due to tight garments or electronics all have a negative impact on spermatogenesis and hormone balance. Ayurvedic focus on a proper āhāra (diet) and vihāra (lifestyle) is totally in line with this contemporary knowledge. In the current clinical regimen, patients were advised to follow diets rich in nutrients and indulgent of Vata Pitta; these modifications probably had a major effect on the noted improvements in sperm quality.

The Jorgensen et al. (2021)[5] study asked a crucial question on a population scale concerning the reducing sperm counts in the world, including the evidence of significant reductions in the last decades and blaming it on environmental toxins and endocrine disruptors, lifestyle shifts, and chronic stress. This macro-level tendency highlights the acuity of preventive and restorative measures. With its emphasis on the long-term balance of doṣhas, agni preservation and dhatus defense, such as that of śukra, Ayurveda can be found a very useful prevention system in this context. The fact that the individual patients have improved in the study can be considered micro-level countermeasures to these global negative trends.

11.5 Vajīkaraṇa, Rasāyana and Reproductive Enhancement

The modern pharmacological evidence of the role of herbal medicines, particularly those that are categorized under Rasasayana (rejuvenative) and Vajikarana (aphrodisiac and fertility-promoting) is very well evidenced. Based on scientifically proven herbal aphrodisiacs, Kotta et al. (2013)[6] provided their positive outcome regarding the effects of these substances on libido, hormone regulation and sperm parameters. Their results are in line with the Ayurvedic tradition of employing plant-based preparations to enhance the quality of Bija (sperm) and treat disorders such as kshina sukra and klaibya. The application of such formulations after purification in the current research seems to have led to improvement of motility, volume and vitality in semen.

Some classical Rasayana herbs have also started to be proved by recent evidence. Oyovwi et al. (2025)[7] emphasized that Shatavari (Asparagus racemosus) can be a valuable fertility-promoting agent in which the authors demonstrated that it has antioxidant, hormonal, and tissue-protective activities applicable to both male and female reproductive health. This is in line with the Ayurvedic description of Shatavari as a dhatu nourishing, cooling Rasanayana that normalises the reproductive tissues and overcomes Pitta and Vata imbalances. On the same note, Akbaribazm et al. (2024)[8] have reviewed the literature on male infertility and herbal medicine in animal models and have shown a consistent increase in the count, motility, and morphology of sperm and decrease in oxidative markers by using Rasayana-like herbs. The reported clinical changes in this research, therefore, fall into an expanding literature that herbal Rasayana and Vajikarana formulae are capable of regulating spermatogenesis and preventing oxidative and inflammatory stress.

11.6 Integrative and Complementary Approaches to Male Infertility

Increasingly, the modality with which male infertility

is treated is known to be inadequate in cases of idiopathic or multifactorial causes, and that integrative approaches are required. Fasanghari et al. (2024)[9] performed an umbrella review and found that complementary and alternative medicine, such as traditional systems such as Ayurveda, may be highly effective in enhancing semen quality and pregnancy outcomes when applied in multimodal protocols. This integrative philosophy is reflected in the intervention design of the current study, which was a combination of Panchakarma-based purification, Rasayana, Vajikarana, dietary control and lifestyle modification. Improvement of semen parameters is substantial, which supports the conclusion that this type of layered interventions can be particularly effective in the case of functional and idiopathic infertility.

Simultaneously, contemporary reproductive medicine has focused attention on the application of antioxidants in order to deal with the oxidative stress. In a Cochrane review, Showell et al. (2014) [10] discovered that antioxidant supplementation of subfertile men positively influenced the semen parameters and the chances of pregnancy were higher in some studies. Such data are in tandem with the Ayurvedic Rasasayana principles of restoring tissue integrity, increasing immunity and postponing degeneration. The clinical results of the current paper indicate that Ayurvedic Rasayana treatment could be an advanced systemic approach based on antioxidants, which might have a more extensive effect than the isolated nutrient supplements, as it affects digestion, mental balance and tissue rejuvenation concomitantly.

11.7 Biochemical and Srotas-Level Interpretation of Findings

Barati et al. (2020)[11] presented an in-depth discussion of the effect of oxidative stress on male fertility, which damages sperm DNA, lipids and proteins, disrupts spermatogenesis and changes the microenvironment of the reproductive tract. They also emphasized the importance of inflammation and oxidative pathways in the testicles and epididymis dysfunction. Such biomedical understanding can be effectively explained by the Ayurvedic term of āma and došhic aggravation that hinders srotases. The significant shortening of the liquidation period and viscosity following the Panchakarma in the present study indicates that the Śodhana treatments have aided in clearing these impediments and normalizing of the internal milieu under which the sperm is produced and transported.

Ayurvedic dietary theory also agrees with this opinion. According toMaharshi Caraka, sweet, unctuous strengthening foods are Rasayana, nourish all the dhatus and are Vrshya, which enhance the integrity of the śukra (Ca. Cikitsāsthāna 2/3).[12] Nutritional and lifestyle prescriptions adopted in the study were well selected to depict these principles hence placing a metabolic background to the effectiveness of cleansing and rejuvenating therapies.

11.8 Classical Doctrines on Śukra, Apāna Vāyu and Śodhana

The Ayurvedic textual corpus offers a very consistent theoretical model on male fertility. Sukra and artava are saumya in their nature that is, cooling and stabilizing and reliant upon the harmonious cooperation of the elements (Su. Śārīrasthāna 3/3).[13] This concept is similar to the current need of accurate thermoregulation, hormonal regulation and microenvironmental stability in the testes and accessory glands to achieve normal spermatogenesis. The imbalance in these parameters, e.g. excessive heat or inflammation, can be easily traced to Pitta aggravation degrading śukra.

Acharya Vagbhahta gives Apana Vayu the control of ejaculation, the movement and the functionality of the pelvic organs (A.H. S. U.S.A. 12/9).[14] This is now in modern physiological terms, the combined interaction of autonomic nervous system, pelvic floor muscles and intra-abdominal pressure underlying ejaculation and semen release. This classical linkage between Apana Vayu equilibrium and reproductive achievement was found in this current experiment in which motility and ejaculatory functioning enhanced with Basti treatment, which is a primary intervention in Vata regulation.

Another point Maharshi Caraka makes is that, disease is caused by the obstruction of the channels (srotas) by doshas and the disruption of the normal flow of the nutrients and wastes. Vimānasthāna 5/8).[15] This principle can be directly used in the case of high semen viscosity, delayed liquefaction and poor motility, in which the motility and functional expression of śukra is obstructed. Acharya Susruta a also states that body that is cleansed does not allow dosha to collect easily and the srotas are clear and, thereby, it is not easy to develop the disease. (Su. Cikitsāsthāna 37/34). [16] The Dipana-Pacana, Snehapana, Virecana and Yogabasti sequence was designed with the sole purpose to provide such purification and clearance of channels and the following clinical improvements confirm the classical expectation.

According to Acharya Vāgbhaṭa, healthy śukra is oily, sweet, radiant and naturally fruit-giving, devoid of doṣha (A.H. Uttarasthana 40/44).[17] These qualitative descriptions are consistent with the current semen attributes that are logical to good fertility, including the right viscosity, normal colour, sufficient volume and reasonable motility. The effectiveness of the multi-stage therapeutic approach in the given work proves this holistic opinion: it was only after purification of channels, mind and tissues were regularly rejuvenated that śukra was restored to its usual amount and properties.

11.9 Summary

A very consistent theoretical base of Ayurvedic male fertility can be created using the classical textual corpus of Ayurveda. Acharya Suruta explains the coolness, stabilizing and reliance of the elements to work harmoniously as soumya of sukras and artava. The concept is similar to the contemporary need of a specific thermoregulation, hormonal equilibrium and in conclusion, the argument proves that the results of the current study match the contemporary biomedical knowledge and classical Ayurvedic concept of male infertility. The role of oxidative stress, lifestyle and psychosocial factors, environmental exposures and minor tissue-level derangements is all critical in undermining sperm functionality. Ayurveda describes these processes in the terms of doṣhas, srotas, agni and śukra dhatu which provide a complete system-based that presupposes a lot of modern findings. The significant changes in the semen parameters seen following a systematic series of Śodhana, Rasayana, Vajikarana, diet and lifestyle control using Ayurveda methods are a clear indication of the therapeutic value of integrative Ayurveda in male infertility treatment and provides encouraging prospects of future clinical investigations and practice.

References

1. Alahmar, A. T. (2019). Role of oxidative stress in male infertility: an updated review. Journal of human reproductive sciences, 12(1), 4-18.

2. Aitken, R. J., & Koppers, A. J. (2010). Apoptosis and DNA damage in human spermatozoa. Asian journal of andrology, 13(1), 36.

3. Nordkap, L., Jensen, T. K., Hansen, Å. M., Lassen, T. H., Bang, A. K., Joensen, U. N., ... & Jørgensen, N. (2016). Psychological stress and testicular function: a cross-sectional study of 1,215 Danish men. Fertility and sterility, 105(1), 174-187.

4. Durairajanayagam, D. (2018). Lifestyle causes of male infertility. Arab journal of urology, 16(1), 10-20.

5. Jørgensen, N., Lamb, D. J., Levine, H., Pastuszak, A. W., Sigalos, J. T., Swan, S. H., & Eisenberg, M. L. (2021). Are worldwide sperm counts declining?. Fertility and Sterility, 116(6), 1457-1463.

6. Kotta, S., Ansari, S. H., & Ali, J. (2013). Exploring scientifically proven herbal aphrodisiacs. Pharmacognosy reviews, 7(13), 1.

7. Oyovwi, M. O., Chijiokwu, E. A., Ben-Azu, B., Ugwuishi, E. W., & Jeroh, E. (2025). Shatavari (Asparagus racemosus): A Promising Ally for Fertility. Current Nutrition Reports, 14(1), 1-13.

8. Akbaribazm, M., Khordad, E., & Rahimi, M. (2024). A Review on Male Infertility and Herbal Medicine: Complementary and Alternative Therapies in Animal Models. OBM Genetics, 8(1), 1-17.

9. Fasanghari, M., Keramat, A., Tansaz, M., Moini, A., & Chaman, R. (2024). Effect of alternative and complementary medicine on male infertility: An umbrella review. Health Science Reports, 7(6), e2118.

10. Showell, M. G., Mackenzie-Proctor, R., Brown, J., Yazdani, A., Stankiewicz, M. T., & Hart, R. J. (2014). Antioxidants for male subfertility. Cochrane Database of Systematic Reviews.

11. Barati, E., Nikzad, H., & Karimian, M. (2020). Oxidative stress and male infertility: current knowledge of

pathophysiology and role of antioxidant therapy in disease management. Cellular and Molecular Life Sciences, 77(1), 93-113.

12. Ca. Cikitsāsthāna 2/3 — Sweet, unctuous foods nourish dhātus and enhance śukra
मधुरं स्निग्धं स्थैर्यबलवर्णकृन्मनःसुखम्।
रसायनं च वृष्यं च सर्वधातुप्रसादनम्।।

13. Su. Śārīrasthāna 3/3 — Śukra is saumya (cool, stabilizing) and vital for reproduction
सौम्यं शुक्रमार्तवमाग्नेयमितरेषाम्।
भूतानां सान्निध्यमत्र परस्परोपकारतः।।

14. A.H. Sūtrasthāna 12/9 — Apāna Vāyu governs ejaculation, semen movement & fertility
अपानोऽपानगः श्रोणिबस्तिमेढ्रोरुगोचरः।

15. Su. Cikitsāsthāna 37/34 — Purification (Śodhana) restores srotas and doṣa balance
शुद्धे शारीरे भवति दोषाणां न निवर्तनम्।
स्रोतसां च विशुद्धानां रोगाणां च न संशयः।।

16. Ca. Vimānasthāna 5/8 — Srotas obstruction (srotorodha) leads to diseases including infertility
स्रोतसां सन्धानविधौ दोषा मार्गान् महान्ति च। तेन स्रोतोविघातेन जायन्ते नान्यथागताः।।

17. A.H. Uttarasthāna 40/44 — Qualities of healthy śukra (śuddha śukra)
स्निग्धं गुरु च मधुरं शुभ्रं वृष्यं च शुक्लकम्। एतद्वीर्यं प्रकीर्तन्ते दोषसङ्करजं विना।।

Chapter - 12

Conclusions

Male infertility and specifically oligospermia is a multifactorial and complicated condition which cuts across the boundaries of physiology, psychology, metabolism, lifestyle, environment and genetics. This state has been analysed in the earlier chapters of this book in the context of both contemporary and Ayurvedic science using the prism of modern and classical science. The results obtained after the conceptual review, clinical observations and case-based evidence enable us to come up with a series of overall conclusions that prove Ayurveda relevance, in-depth and treatment ability in the context of male infertility. The integrative model that created during this work - which includes the physiology of the Śukra Dhātu, the theory of dosas, the pathology of srotas, Panchakarma, Rasayana, Vajikarana, the Ahara-Vihara, psychosocial care, etc. - proves that, the reproductive health is not a solitary action but the result of a very interconnected system. The conclusion of the written evidence and clinical outcomes in Chapter 9 confirm the point that once this system is holistically restored, the semen parameters and reproductive vitality would improve significantly.

The first key finding of this work is that, Ayurveda provides a complex and yet exceedingly detailed approach to the investigation of the male reproductive physiology and that it is similar to contemporary scientific theories in many aspects, yet adds some further dimensions of the understanding. The classical explanation of Śukra Dhātu as the last and the finest of all the seven dhatus describes the fact that the quality of semen is closely associated with the digestion, metabolism, mood and general well-being. This conceptualization is already present in modern systemic interpretations of fertility, which also include the role of endocrine health, metabolic health, oxidative stress, nutrition and psychological stability in spermatogenesis. The Ayurvedic classification of visible (vyakta) and invisible (avyakta) śukra is beneficial to feed our sense as it implies that the principle of reproductive essence is dispersed throughout the body affecting energy, mood, immunity and strength. This holistic style has been confirmed by modern studies which indicated that the quality of sperms reflects the general metabolic and mental wellbeing of a man. This way, the ancient Ayurvedic principles are not only in line with, but also in significant aspects, complementary to modern interpretation of male infertility.

The second conclusion is associated with the overlap of Ayurvedic etiological models and contemporary medical biomedical criteria of infertility. There are various causes that modern science has identified as causes of it including a disruption of the endocrine system, dysfunction of testicles, anatomical obstruction, infections, oxidative stress, environmental toxins and lifestyle practices. These disturbances are categorized into doṣha vitiation, agnimandya, āma accumulation, srotorodha, bīja duṣti and kshina shukra by Ayurveda. There is a lot of overlap of these frameworks. Vata imbalances are related to the motility disorders and ejaculatory dysfunction; Pitta imbalances are associated with an oxidative damage and morphological abnormalities; Kapha imbalances are similar to the conditions of viscosity, stagnation and low liquefaction. Similarly, srotorodha is directly applied onto the obstructive pathology, whereas ama indicates inflammatory alterations, pH disturbance, leukocytospermia and malfunctioning viscosity. Ayurvedic theory of bija dushti is similar to the modern research on sperm DNA fragmentation and genetic abnormalities. This synthesis that Ayurveda offers a more systemic and detailed explanation of male infertility that involves subtle imbalances that are not always easy to discern in purely biomedical models. It is noted in this work that the application of the two systems together gets a more holistic diagnostic and treatment method.

The third key conclusion is based on the clinical results: the organised Panchakarma-Rasayana-Vajikarana regimen has significant and quantifiable benefits on the seminal parameters of men with oligospermia and asthenozoospermia. The three reported cases were treated with the same sequential procedure that showed significant improvement in all the measured variables, such as sperm concentration, motility, liquefaction time, viscosity and volume. Such results confirm the claims that before therapeutic effects to be maximally effective, purification (Śodhana) has to happen before rejuvenation (Rasayana) and Vajikarana. Dipana-Pacana replenished digestive fire and minimized āma, which enhanced the assimilation of nutrients. Snehapana and Swedana aroused ingrained doshas. Virecana was effective in removing Pitta impurities that cause semen defects at qualitative levels. Yoga Basti corrected Vata imbalance, enhanced pelvic circulation, balanced Apana Vayu and adjusted ejaculatory functionality of the body directly affecting patterns of motility and liquefaction. Rasayana and Vajikarana preparations post-purification then targeted to nourish the hormone-producing tissue of the body, hormonal balance and regeneration of reproductive tissues. The dramatic changes in motility up to 80 percent in Case 2 and the tripling of the count in all cases, are the most empirical evidence of the multi-layered Ayurveda therapeutic system and of the classical saying that the finest soil is a purified body in which to begin rejuvenation.

The fourth conclusion made on the psychosocial and behavioural perspective is that the mind is equally crucial in causing male infertility and its therapeutic control cannot be ignored. Ayurveda has continued to highlight the importance of manas, sattva and vayu especially apana vayu in the management of libido, erection, ejaculation and movement of semen. Classical descriptions are reflected in current findings which indicate that stress interferes with HPG axis functions, reduces testosterone and elevates oxidative load and decreases sperm-making. The men referred in the case series reported of being stressed, having poor sleep, irregular routines or emotional exhaustion- all of which worsened Vata and further led to their reproductive dysfunction. After Panchakarma, psychological condition, sleep patterns, digestion and clarity of thinking were also observed to improve along with the semen quality. This supports the idea that counselling, Satvavajaya Cikitsa, yoga, pranayama and lifestyle correction are not secondary elements but major treatment methods. Pharmacological treatment of male infertility cannot be taken exclusively into consideration; emotional recovery and reorganization of behaviour are necessary and affect the outcome in relation to the reproductive success.

The fifth conclusion is the importance of diet (Āhāra) and lifestyle (Vihāra) which is indispensable to restore fertility. Classical works are all in agreement that the quality of sperm is determined by healthy diet, good digestion and regular habits. Diets rich in incompatible, dense, dry, over spicy or dry types of foods cause dosha imbalance, srotas obstruction and hindrance of semen formation. The contemporary analogies are inappropriate nutrition and obesity, taking of alcohol, eating processed foods and nutritional deficiencies. The case studies have validated that patients having erratic diets or constipation had more sluggish and viscous semen. Treatment of Āhāra and Vihāra greatly improved the effectiveness of the treatment protocol. Therapies based on stable agni and clear srotas such as Rasayana and Vajikarana therapies became effective at a deeper level in cases where the lifestyle basis had been rectified. Therefore, an essential finding is that the long-term reproductive health is maintained by neither the herbal preparations itself but by the regularity of diet control, moderation in sexual activity, sleep, emotional control and daily conscious life.

One of the sixth conclusions of this study is that the strength of Ayurveda is that it could treat functional infertility which in most cases does not have clear biomedical pathology but has apparent reproductive impairment. The three cases in Chapter 9 were non-obstructive and functional infertility, having normal imaging, normal blood tests, no structural defects, but persistent oligospermia or asthenospermia. Such patients are usually grouped under the heading of idiopathic in the context of modern medicine, and the therapeutic treatment provided is minimal. However, Ayurveda explains such nuances by agni, dosha, and srotas imbalances, which makes possible specific, personalized, and comprehensive treatment. The fact that these cases were successful thus indicates that Ayurveda has the potential to bridge a significant therapeutic gap in functional infertility a phenomenon where conventional medicine is still lagging.

Last, the general conclusion is that Ayurveda has offered an integrative, multidimensional and evidence-based and clinically effective paradigm of management of male infertility particularly in asthenozoospermia and oligospermia. The subtle imbalances can be observed through its systemic vision; the profoundness of the procedure can be purifying; the rejuvenating effectiveness can be tissue-forming on the ground; and the sensitivity of the psychosocial life on the emotional and relational level. They are complementary to Ayurvedic knowledge because modern diagnostic techniques, including semen analysis and imaging, are not in competition with Ayurvedic wisdom. Combining the two systems brings an outcome of developing an improved therapeutic system that has the potential to achieve significant changes and sustainable reproductive health.

Overall, in this book, tried to show that the classical Ayurvedic system based on the millennia-old wisdom and confirmed by the current clinical results offers a potent and holistic approach to male infertility treatment founded on its scientific basis. The meeting point of textual authority, conceptual depth and empirical evidence are what makes Ayurveda so highly relevant over time and how it can be transformed so effectively indeed when carefully blended with contemporary reproductive science. In conclusion, this piece of writing confirms that the fertility does not simply mean the power to conceive but the manifestation of a balanced mind, a nourished body, a harmonious metabolism and a steady inner world. Once these factors are revitalized, reproductive vitality is naturally developed as observed in the outcomes of clinical successes and natural conception recorded in the study.

Appendices

Appendix 14.1 – Glossary of Sanskrit Terminology

Sanskrit Term	Definition / Explanation
Āgantu Doṣa	External perturbations of doṣhas due to toxins, trauma, microbes, chemicals, or environmental exposures.
Agnimāndya	Weak digestive/metabolic fire causing impaired digestion, poor nutrient assimilation, and formation of āma.
Āhāra	Diet and nutrition; foundational determinant of dhātu formation and śukra quality.
Āma	Metabolic toxin from incomplete digestion; obstructs srotas and impairs semen quality.
Apāna Vāyu	Subtype of Vāta governing ejaculation, pelvic organ function, semen movement, urination, defecation.
Bīja	"Seed"; refers to sperm or ovum, including genetic essence (phenotype + genotype).
Bīja Duṣṭi	Defective sperm/ovum; corresponds to DNA fragmentation, genetic abnormalities, altered morphology.

Bṛṃhaṇa	Tissue-building and nourishing therapy; increases strength and fertility.
Cikitsā	General word for therapy or treatment.
Cikitsāsthāna	Treatment section of classical Ayurvedic texts (Caraka, Suśruta, Aṣṭāṅga Hṛdayam).
Doṣha	Functional principles governing physiology (Vāta, Pitta, Kapha).
Doṣa Duṣṭi	Vitiation of doṣhas leading to disease and infertility.
Dhātu	Seven body tissues; śukra is the final, most refined tissue.
Jatharāgni	Central digestive fire controlling food digestion and nourishment of tissues.
Kapha	Doṣa governing stability, lubrication, and semen viscosity.
Klaibya	Sexual dysfunction including impotence, ejaculatory weakness, infertility.
Kṣhīṇa Śukra	Weak/low semen (quantity or quality); correlates with oligospermia/asthenospermia.
Laṅghana	Lightening therapy including fasting, improving metabolism, reducing āma.
Manas	Mind; affects reproductive function through stress, emotions, and vata regulation.
Pañcakarma	Five purification therapies (Vamana, Virecana, Basti, Nasya, Raktamokṣaṇa).

Pitta	Doṣa responsible for metabolism, heat, enzymatic activity, and oxidative processes.
Rasāyana	Rejuvenative therapy that enhances vitality, immunity, longevity, and sperm quality.
Rasa Dhātu	Primary nutrient fluid that nourishes all tissues including śukra.
Śodhana	Purification therapy to remove doṣhas and clear srotas (e.g. Virecana, Basti).
Śukra Dhātu	Reproductive tissue; includes visible semen and subtle reproductive vitality.
Śukra Duṣṭi	Qualitative abnormalities in semen; relates to functional infertility.
Śukravaha Srotas	Channels involved in the production, nourishment, and movement of śukra.
Snehapāna	Internal oleation to mobilize doṣhas before purification.
Srotas	Body channels transporting nutrients/wastes; crucial for fertility.
Srotorodha	Blockage of channels; associated with high viscosity, low motility.
Tejas	Subtle essence of metabolism closely linked to cell

14.2 Charts, Flowcharts & Algorithmic Management Pathways

14.2.1 Master Flowchart

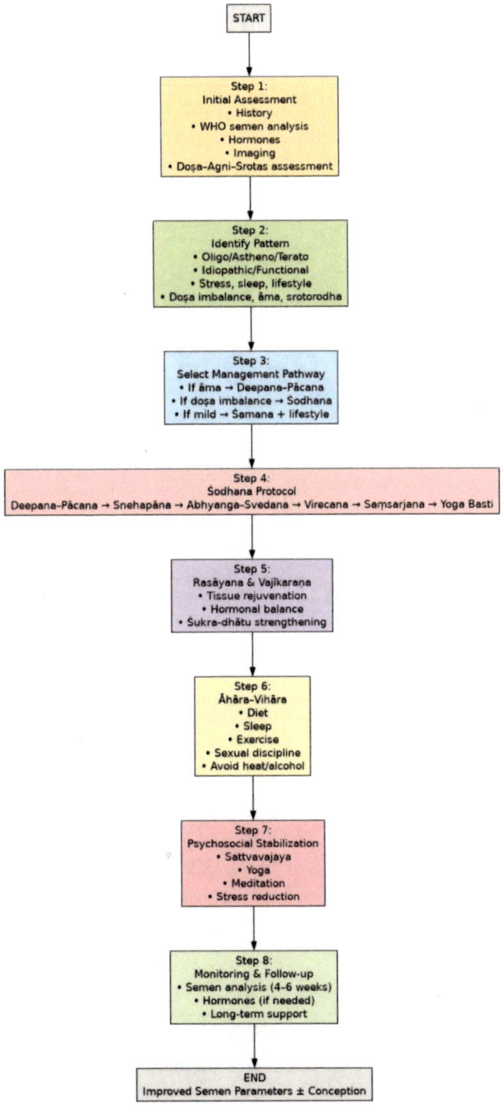

14.2.2 Panchakarma Treatment Flowchart

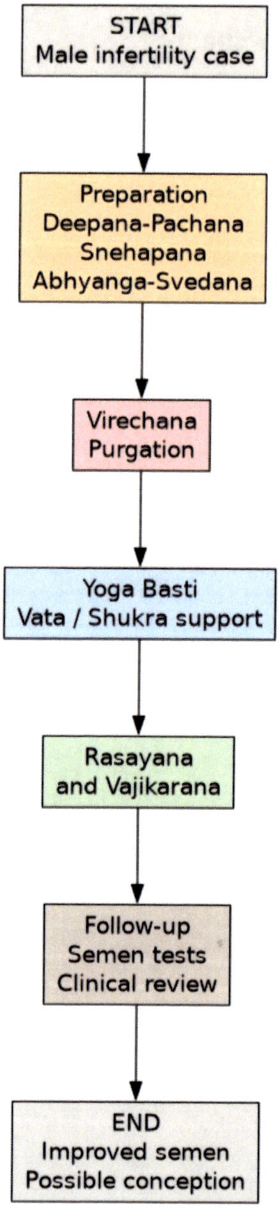

14.2.3 Lifestyle Correction Blueprint

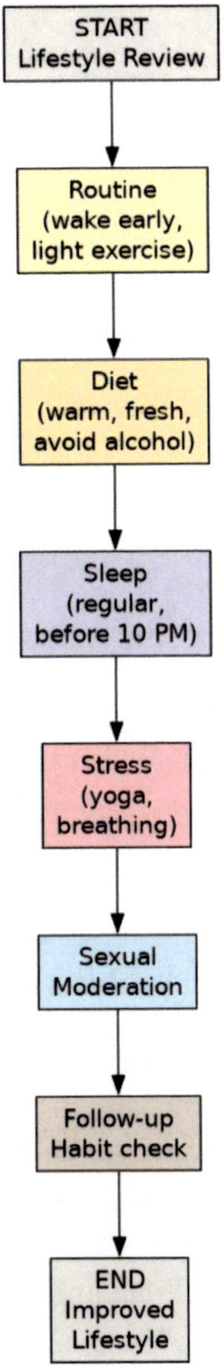

14.2.4 Algorithm: Ayurvedic Interpretation of Semen Abnormalities

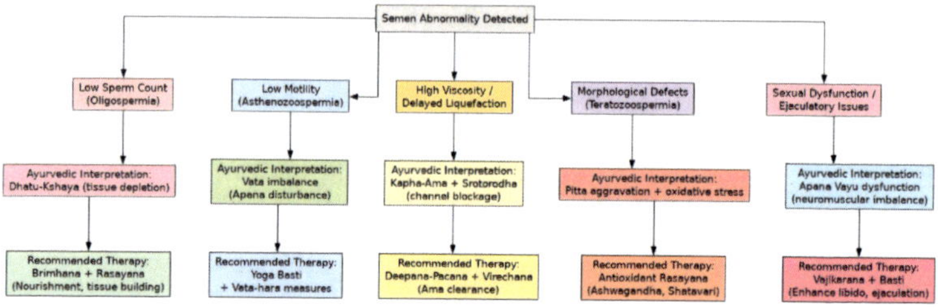

14.3 Additional Resources for Clinicians and Researchers

A curated list of high-value sources for integrative reproductive healthcare.

14.3.1 Classical Ayurvedic Texts

- Caraka Saṃhitā (Critical Edition, any translation)
- Aṣṭāṅga Hṛdaya (K.R. Srikantha Murthy's translation recommended)
- Suśruta Saṃhitā
- Kāśyapa Saṃhitā (for reproductive guidance)

14.3.2 Modern Semen Analysis & Clinical Guidelines

- WHO Manual for Human Semen Examination (5th and 6th editions)
- European Association of Urology (EAU) Male Infertility Guidelines
- AUA–ASRM Male Infertility Guidelines
- Lancet Review on Male Infertility (2021)

14.3.3 Key Modern Research Areas for Integrative Fertility

- Oxidative stress biomarkers (ROS, TAC, SDF)
- Endocrine disruptors and reproductive epigenetics
- Lifestyle intervention studies (exercise, sleep, stress)
- Antioxidant clinical trials
- Herbal pharmacology & Rasāyana mechanisms
- Psychosomatic medicine in male infertility
- Ayurvedic diagnostic pattern research (doṣa/agnimāndya/srotas mapping)

14.3.4 Phytopharmacology Resources

- Indian Materia Medica
- API (Ayurvedic Pharmacopoeia of India)
- Rasamruta, Yogaratnākara
- Research monographs on Ashwagandha, Shatavari, Gokshura, Shilajit, Kapikacchu

14.3.5 Useful Databases

- PubMed
- AYUSH Research Portal
- DHARA (Digital Helpline for Ayurveda Research Articles)
- Google Scholar
- Scopus
- ResearchGate

14.3.6 Tools for Clinicians

- Semen analysis interpretation charts
- Lifestyle counselling templates

- Stress profiling scales
- Diet planning modules for śukra-vardhaka regimens
- Panchakarma protocol checklists
- Follow-up monitoring sheets (every 4–6 weeks)